SIMON SAYS

# LOVE
## YOUR
# LEGACY

A Guide to Financial Education
for You and Your Family

BY

# SAUL M. SIMON
CFP®, CFS, RFC

# DEDICATION

◆

THIS BOOK IS DEDICATED to my parents Marjorie and Stuart Simon. Thank you, mom and dad, for your unconditional love and support, and for the many lessons in communication that you taught my brothers and me. In addition, congratulations on celebrating 53 years together. You're both such an awesome example of what it takes to communicate, and be committed to love, honor and work through the normal ups and downs of a relationship and life in general.

My brothers Craig, Brian and Marc, thank you for your partnership, love and support. Knowing you are in my corner in life has been an incredible comfort.

To my one and only, Uncle Jerry, my mentor and confidant. Your continued words of encouragement, guidance and love cannot be expressed in words. You're like an older brother to me, and I'm grateful for our relationship.

Thanks to my children Danielle and Jack for teaching me on a daily basis about myself and how to see life through your eyes. You mean the world to me and I love and appreciate you both every single day.

In memory of my main squeeze Grandma Molly and Aunt Brenda —I miss you very much and know you are here with me always.

To my many friends and supporters over the years. This has been a dream come true, and I thank you from the bottom of my heart for all that you've contributed to my life both personally and professionally.

Lastly, to the many families who struggle to communicate with their children, siblings, nieces, nephews, or cousins with whom they may not have relationship, I hope this book can provide access to open a dialogue that can repair what's most important to you.

I wish you good health, love, and happiness in the ways that matter most to you. As I've learned through my life experiences and from taking educational courses through landmark education, life is short, so don't sweat the small stuff and focus on what matters most.

With love,
*Saul*

# CONTENTS

◆

# ABOUT THE AUTHOR

◆

A S A CERTIFIED FINANCIAL PLANNER™ Practitioner for over twenty years and president of Simon Financial Group, Saul M. Simon specializes in working with individuals and business owners to develop strategic financial plans that help them reach their financial and family objectives. Through a deep understanding of his clients' goals and objectives, he helps to develop a sense of long-term confidence even through the vicissitudes of financial markets and changing economies.

A strong believer in financial education, Saul sponsors lectures on financial planning for corporations, adult education programs, and community organizations. He also hosts a TV program called "Simon Says Manage Your Money," and has appeared as a guest with CNBC, Fox Business, One on One/Caucus NJ with Steve Adubato, Ebru Today, and Local NY Affiliates Fox 5 and WOR 9.

A graduate of William Paterson University and the College for Financial Planning, Saul is a board member of the Henry Kessler Foundation, The Bass Foundation, and Temple B'nai Jeshurun.

◆

# PREFACE

◆

BENJAMIN FRANKLIN SAID that in life two things are certain: death and taxes.

It is unfortunate that these two subjects are among the most difficult to discuss with our brothers, sisters, spouse, children, or grandchildren. But it's a conversation that is more important than ever. We live in a time of an historic transfer of post-World War Two wealth from grandparents to their children and then to the grandchildren. And because of our love for our children, and perhaps because of our own feeling of having struggled when we were young, we may spoil our kids. We may even unintentionally create in our children a sense of entitlement. Regardless of the choices they make, they may grow up to expect a certain level of material comfort and income.

Choices can have consequences. Most of us are too young to remember the Great Depression of the 1930s, which our parents or grandparents experienced; but all of us are still living through the next worse economic event of our times—the Great Recession. We know that fortunes can be lost, debt can be very bad, and you never know what tomorrow may bring.

As for me, I don't come from money. I'm a saver. To gain airline miles I use my credit card for everything, and I'm adamant about paying off the credit card at the end of the month. If I don't have the money, I don't spend it. I have three younger brothers, and I grew up with the attitude that the family had to stick together. When I was a kid I had a paper route and I sold fruit to qualify to attend a senior class trip to Orlando, Florida. My dad had lost his job and our family experienced hard times; at one point I remember collecting food stamps, so I'm very conscientious about money. Perhaps it's no coincidence that today I'm a financial advisor and I have my own business.

I'm passionate about education, contribution and making a difference in people's lives. I'm upset when consumers have to pay the exorbitant interest rates that banking institutions charge. And when the bank savings accounts are paying us less than one percent interest, I think it's theft and I'm outraged by it.

I wrote *Simon Says: Love Your Legacy* for some very practical personal reasons. I'm a single father with two children and the possibility of a future extended nuclear family. I've also factored in the possibility of stepchildren and the current rate of divorce being over fifty percent. Families can be messy, and in my professional work I too often see the same scenario: only after a sickness or a death do family members assemble for a frank discussion about finances. It's always after the fact, when emotions are running high. Why not get together beforehand? Why not create conversation beforehand? Why not tell our children *now* what our intentions are? Why wait to assist and manage the relationship, and more importantly the feeling that will arise from the disposition of assets and duties?

For example, let's say you have four surviving children. You love each of them. When you become incapacitated or die, who will be in charge of your legacy? The oldest? Or number three? To ensure your legacy is passed smoothly to your heirs, you need a structure already in place. Everybody must know that upon the onset of a terminal sickness or after death, this person is the trustee, this person is the fiduciary, this is the executor/executrix, this is my power of attorney, and this is my living will healthcare advocate.

This discussion and education should start early. I want you to share the lessons of this book with your children and grandchildren, and discuss with them these concepts of money and value in language that is simple and easy to understand. I want you to engage in conversation, share your values and your vision as to where you came from, and discuss your thoughts about money and other assets. It's to help them understand what money is—what it's worth, what it can buy, and how it can be either conserved or wasted. It can be a discussion that helps your family value and appreciate your legacy and not take it for granted.

In this way, you—and your family—can truly love your legacy.

*Saul M Simon*

# INTRODUCTION

◆

# NOTES

# Introduction

◆

SIMON SAYS, "LOVE YOUR LEGACY."
What does this mean?

*Simon Says: Love Your Legacy* means being smart about passing your assets to your heirs. It means taking steps to ensure that your heirs understand the value of money and know how to wisely use and manage your accumulated wealth.

Perhaps even more importantly it means being able to stamp out the word "entitlement" and create a meaningful dialogue about a sensitive subject.

*Simon Says: Love Your Legacy* is about money, wisdom, experience, entitlement issues, and that retiring rich doesn't have to be all about money. It's about sharing wisdom, sharing experience from grandfather to grandchild, and having them understand where they came from and how you made your money. It may even be just about saying, "Are you okay?"

It's also about acknowledging that conflict can arise among parents and children, siblings, aunts and uncles, or cousins. Sometimes it's unavoidable, but it's always better to plan in advance so that conflicts can be managed if not ameliorated to who you want, when you want, and the manner you want.

We all want the next generation to be able to prosper from the experiences and lessons that our parents and grandparents learned; and we, as parents and grandparents, want to give this gift to them.

It's not just about how to pass along a big pile of cash. Your legacy may be real estate, a business, a treasured work of art, or even grandma's antique engagement ring. It may be your outlook on life. It's whatever has value to you.

But how do you do it? How do you facilitate this passing of your wisdom onto them?

To these and other questions, *Simon Says: Love Your Legacy* provides the answers.

I'll show you how to begin the kind of conversation that you may feel is awkward or you don't know how to create. In a series of easy-to-understand chapters, *Simon Says: Love Your Legacy* will reveal my secrets for opening up a discussion and removing discomfort.

The book is organized into the seven overall topics of education, saving, spending, making your money grow, planning ahead, trusts, and writing your will. Within each topic I present key information that will help you to educate your heirs and set up a structure so that your legacy will be honored and appreciated.

I'll cover how to talk to your kids about your legacy, educate them about charities, and discuss the wisdom of building an emergency fund. My tips will cover life insurance, financial planning, setting up trusts, and choosing a trustee and executor. I'll discuss writing your will and how to prepare for the possibility of unhappy heirs.

We'll cover the basics of 401(k) plans, college savings plans, how to open a Roth IRA, and much more.

With my easy-to-use format, you can pick the topics that apply to you and your family. *Simon Says: Love Your Legacy* is written for anyone who hopes to leave assets to one or more heirs, whether it's that special piece of heirloom jewelry, real estate, securities, a business, or a nest egg for college. Whether it's simple or complex, your legacy is important to you, and this book can help you pass it to your heirs.

With *Simon Says: Love Your Legacy* you'll learn how to say, "This is where I come from and this is what I've done to amass the wealth that I'm ready to share with you. And I believe that you're entitled to straight talk, and that you're ready to accept responsibility for my legacy and to make it a part of your own."

Ready? I invite you to read *Simon Says: Love Your Legacy,* and then call a family meeting so that you can lay the groundwork for a successful and loving transfer of your legacy to the generations that follow.

# EDUCATION

◆

# NOTES

# SIMON SAYS:
# TALK TO YOUR KIDS

◆

THERE ARE TWO WAYS to go about passing your financial legacy on to your children or grandchildren.

The first is to make your will, and after your death they can read the will and discover what you left for them.

The second way is to make your children part of the process. Educate them and work with them so that they understand the value of your legacy and appreciate the context in which it is given to them. Make them not merely recipients but stewards.

You know which choice Simon says makes the most sense.

It's unfortunate that in many families, money is a topic that's deemed off limits. Combine that with another unpopular topic—death—and you often have a toxic area that no one will touch. Talking about family finances, even to one's own children, makes some parents deeply anxious.

And the more money there is at stake, the more difficult the conversation can become. Lack of open communication about money can be especially prevalent in wealthier households, where parents are afraid that the concepts of inherited wealth and self-sufficiency are mutually exclusive. If you reveal to your child the extent of his or her inheritance, the child may become lazy or simply tread water until the windfall arrives. (Of course, with today's life expectancies, your kids may have a very long wait!)

Here are six strategies that can help you frame the discussion with your kids. (I'm keeping this simple):

1. **Set a good example.** Your children will learn to manage finances more effectively if they see you doing the same. For example, don't just go out and buy a new wide-screen TV with your credit card.

Involve your kids in the purchase by having them comparison shop. Set up a savings fund and set a goal for a budgeted price. If they're young, pay them for simple chores and put the payments in the savings fund. Of course you'll be planning on footing 95% of the cost, but their involvement in the process will show them the value of saving and they'll have more appreciation for the TV.

2. **Give your kids an allowance**. Kids can learn good financial habits from receiving an allowance, however, don't just hand them cash every Saturday morning. Structure the allowance program to teach your children important money lessons. Set up a passbook savings account and go with them to the bank to deposit a portion of their allowance every week. Let them see how their savings increases over time. When the bank statement comes in the mail addressed to you and your child, Simon says to share this with them so that they can obtain a sense of responsibility and ownership. It will also make them proud and feel good about themselves.

3. **Start young.** It's never too early to talk to your children about money. Even when they're in first grade, learning about money is a great way to master basic math skills and begin to understand the relationship between something they see in a store and paying with money. When they want to purchase a new doll, sneakers, boots, videogames, bicycle, make sure they see how much money it costs, and you can even point out how much the item costs relative to other things. Have them play store at home, with a little cash register and grocery items.

4. **Start old**. Here's the flip side to tip #3: It's never too late to talk to your children about money. You can discuss college finances with your high school grad. You can talk about home finance with your newlywed son or daughter. You can talk about a trust fund for your first grandchild. If you've never talked about money before with your kids, break the ice! You'll be glad you did.

5. **Learn how to talk in generalities**. Children don't need to know exactly how much you and your spouse earn or your family's net worth, but that doesn't mean questions about money should be avoided. For example, if you're discussing the family vacation budget, you can say, "Our household operates on approximately one hundred thousand dollars a year. Out of this, we can spend about five thousand on our vacation. Here are some of the places we can go for two weeks. Or would you guys rather go on a short trip and save some of the vacation fund to add it to next year's trip?" And make sure that the kids understand that the value of assets such as stocks can fluctuate considerably in value over time.

6. **Link your assets with your personal financial values**. How do you use your money? On gambling trips to Vegas, or investing in home improvements? Your children will be less likely to take money for granted and make financial mistakes if they understand how your values and beliefs are reflected in your financial behavior. This is revealed in how you earn your money (through work), spend your money (thoughtfully), and support the community through charitable giving.

## SIMON SAYS...

The most important thing is to start the conversation. When your kids are young, make it fun and easy. If they're adults, sit down over a nice dinner and a bottle of wine. Be honest. Whether they're your biological children, adopted, or stepchildren, give them the straight story. Say, "I'm not going to tell you every detail of my financial life, but I want you to be aware of your place in the family, and your rights and responsibilities." You—and they—will be glad you did.

◆

# SIMON SAYS:
# GIVE TO CHARITY

◆

ONE OF THE MOST IMPORTANT LESSONs you can teach your children and grandchildren is that charities do many good things that you cannot do yourself.

Ask them to think about what a charity organization such as the United Way, the American Red Cross, or the Salvation Army is able to accomplish to help those in need. You certainly can't go out and collect blood, process it, and get it to hospitals for patients. You couldn't provide hot meals to 200 or 2,000 senior citizens in their homes every day.

Fortunately for you and for me, there are wonderful charitable organizations in our society, with dedicated people using the dollars we donate to accomplish great things for our fellow human beings that we as individuals cannot do.

## How to Make Your Donations

The first thing you need to know is that legitimate charitable organizations are designated by the IRS as 503(c) tax-exempt entities. To be considered as a nonprofit, charitable, or religious organization, the group must apply for that status to the IRS. When it's granted, the organization is then called a 503(c) organization. This means that when you donate money or assets to them, your donation can be deducted from your federal income tax return.

Before you donate money to any charity, make sure it has the 503(c) designation. And get a receipt, year-end statement, or cancelled check as a record of your donation.

There are currently no restrictions as to the amount of money or size of your donation to a church, college, or other 503(c) organization.

Before you write a large, generous check to your favorite charity, consider making a donation of stock instead. Let's say that you have some stock that has had significant appreciation, and today it's worth $50 per share. When you gift a hundred shares of that stock—a value of $5,000 to the charity—you'll get a tax deduction based on the current stock market value of those shares, or $5,000.

The charity can then turn around and sell the stock to get cash with no tax consequences.

However, if you sold the stock to receive $5,000 cash to donate to the charity, and your cost basis was $1,000, you would incur a capital gains tax which is currently 20%, or in this example, $800. So you would end up having only $4,200 to donate.

($5000-1000=4000 ➜ 20%= 800 ➜ 5000-800= $4,200)

Don't give to every charity that asks you; you can't afford it. Instead, choose ones that have a special meaning to you and your family.

Also, think about where your donation may have the most impact. Let's say, for example, that you have $5,000 to donate. You could give it to the American Heart Association, or you could donate it to your town's volunteer ambulance service or senior citizen center. The seniors will use your donation to purchase ten new computers for the center. The ambulance squad will purchase a portable defibrillator to keep at the center. The American Heart Association will combine your donation with thousands of others to fund important research and valuable educational programs. Your gift of $5,000 will benefit all of those organizations. Where do you want it to have the most impact? (Start this conversation with your children)

Before you give to a charity that you're not familiar with, check it out first. You can call the local Better Business Bureau or your state's Attorney General's office. You can use the Internet; go to the Better Business Bureau Wise Giving Alliance at http://www.give.org. There you'll find detailed information about the organization's purpose, how the group achieves its goals, and how much of your dollar is used for true charitable purposes. You'll also find more tips on giving.

Never make a pledge or donation based solely on a telephone request you receive. Legitimate organizations certainly make phone calls requesting donations, but you can ask them to mail you more information that you can read carefully before you make a commitment to give. Legitimate organizations will be happy to send you printed materials. Be wary if the caller says, "We don't have any literature to mail to you," or "We don't have time to mail you something," or "We can't afford the postage," or "We'll have someone drop off some literature at your home this afternoon."

## SIMON SAYS...

Remember, please, that charities do wonderful work to help the poor, the homeless, the elderly, the abused, the children, and others in need. They do the work that you and I can't do or don't know how to do. Set a good example for your family by giving as much as you can— and remember you get a tax break for helping.

◆

# SIMON SAYS: GIVE YOUR CHILDREN AN ALLOWANCE

◆

IT'S IMPORTANT THAT WE HELP our kids learn and practice good money management skills from an early age.

Children whose parents lived during the Great Depression undoubtedly heard over and over again as they grew up what it was like to have no money, no job, and no savings. You, too, may have been raised with a continuing explanation and discussion in your home of how to earn, manage, and save money, perhaps even starting when you were a child.

Even so, there are millions of baby boomers today on whom the lesson has been lost and who do not have sufficient savings for retirement.

It can be difficult to change the attitude and money management strategies you've been using all of your life. That's why it's so important to start teaching your children about money and money management very early in life—Simon Says start right now.

## Allowance or No Allowance?
## Is that the Question?

You'll find books, magazine articles, and websites offering many strategies and suggestions to help your child learn to manage and save money. The debate in many of these approaches seems to focus on whether or not you should give your child an allowance.

Should you give a weekly or monthly amount without restrictions? Should you require certain chores be done for that allowance? Should there be no allowance—only "pay" for the "work" your child does around the house, such as keeping his or her room clean, walking the dog, mowing the lawn, and so on, with "performance bonuses" for good grades or taking on additional responsibilities?

Or should your child have to work and contribute his or her share to the household chores without any compensation—just as mom and dad do?

Experts have differing opinions and explanations as to why they believe each method works or doesn't work. I'm not going to throw my opinions into the debate. You'll know which strategy fits best with you, your family, your child, and your own perception of money and how it is acquired. Any of the "expert" ideas can work very well. I want instead to focus on the next step.

## Better Question: How Will Your Child "Get the Message?"

Once your child has the allowance, pay, or whatever you wish to call it, the real skill of money management comes into play. What will he or she do with the money? How will your child manage his or her income?

Here's a plan that I especially like because it's simple, because it incorporates all of the key provisions of wise money management, and because it's easy for even a young child to understand.

Agree with your child that his or her weekly or monthly allowance will be divided into quarters. Each quarter has a specific purpose:

♦ One quarter is for the child to spend for "immediate gratification."

♦ One quarter goes into a savings account to save for a significant purchase—a bicycle, a car, new skis.

♦ One quarter goes into another account to save for college—preferably into a 529 College Savings Plan, discussed in the Chapter Making Your Money Grow.

◆ One Quarter goes to a charity of the child's choice.

As an added incentive, you may want to consider matching the child's savings—dollar for dollar or fifty cents per dollar—just as many 401(k) plans do or used to. You can match either or both the "significant purchase" account and the college savings account.

Decide up front how your plan will deal with cash gifts your child may receive for birthdays and holidays. Should they be divided in the same manner?

With both savings methods, your child will get regular statements, showing his or her deposits, your matching funds, and any interest or dividends that are being earned. Reviewing the statement and pointing out the positive results—the growing value of the account—is an excellent way to reinforce your lessons.

"See, honey?" you'll say. "It works!"

## Is it too Late to Start Teaching Your Teen?

A growing number of public schools are now offering—even requiring—students to take a basic Personal Finances course before they graduate from high school. It's a good idea, but its impact may be muted if your teen has had access to money and has been free to spend it any way he or she wants, without guidelines, restrictions, or incentives for savings, and if you've been generous by giving him or her almost everything he or she has asked for.

There is, however, a good strategy that I've heard about and want to share with you that may at least get the message about the importance of managing money across to your teen, if not the long-term habit of saving money.

You and your teen make a list of everything he or she needs money for during a typical month. Include school lunches, bus or subway fare, school supplies, clothing, school trips, video games, cellphones, parties and movies, hair cuts, gas and auto insurance for the car—everything! Then add it up. Your teen will be surprised at how much money he or she needs every month.

In most families, you've been the source of this monthly "income" for your teen and you'll continue to be the primary source as long as he or she is not working full-time.

Here's the strategy.

On the first day of each month, give your teen the total amount he or she will need for the entire month, or once a week based on the list you've made and agreed upon. He or she may no longer ask you for money; you will *not* give any extra if asked.

Your teen now has to budget and get along solely on that monthly amount. He or she may have to apportion part of each month's allotment for a large upcoming expense such as a prom dress, tuxedo rental, or limousine rental.

Expect that the first month or two, your teen will run out of money well before the end of the month. Check to be sure he or she isn't skipping school lunches, and carefully monitor required payments such as those for auto insurance payments.

Within three months, I can almost guarantee you that your teen will have a better understanding and appreciation for the value of money. He or she will make better spending decisions and will begin to save for upcoming expenses. He or she will finally understand what you've been saying all along: "Money doesn't grow on trees!" There isn't an endless supply. It has to be managed.

Nobody can teach your child about money—what it is, where it comes from, what it brings, how and why it should be saved—as well as *you* can. You, the parent, are the most influential person in your child's life. Take advantage of that special relationship to give your child one of life's most important, long-lasting lessons.

You aren't doing your child a favor by "bailing him out" every time he needs money for something, by giving her the money for a haircut, a trip to the mall, or paying his or her auto insurance premiums every month. It's a sign of your true love and caring for your child to help him or her learn to manage money wisely.

Maybe "tough love" is needed. If your teen has to "sink or swim"—do without something for a while or borrow and have to repay money to a friend—it's better that it happens now, while he or she is a minor without serious negative consequences. Otherwise, your adult children will make poor decisions that could affect them for the rest of their life—overspending, using high-interest credit cards, racking up huge amounts of debt, and ruining their credit rating so that they won't be able to buy a home or purchase a car.

I recently presented a workshop to my son's fifth grade class and came upon this free educational comic book about money. I think it's so important to teach our legacy about smart financial skills.

**http://practicalmoneyskills.com/avengers/**
**Avengers Comic Teaches Mad Money Skills.**
Join the Avengers and a special guest in this exciting educational comic about saving money and saving the day. The heroes team up to defeat Mole Man and his evil army, all while learning important financial skills. The action-packed comic features a budgeting work-sheet, finance terms and more.

PS. This youtube segment also highlights some financial tips on teaching your kids the value of money. I hope it's helpful.
**http://www.youtube.com/watch?v=nNx9h92MABc**

## SIMON SAYS...
Learning to save, spend, and manage money is one of the best gifts you can give your child. Don't wait another minute to start!

◆

# SAVINGS

◆

# NOTES

# SIMON SAYS:
# PAY YOURSELF FIRST

◆

EVER WONDER WHY SOME PEOPLE have the money to buy a home, to take a cruise, or to retire and play golf every day? These people didn't win the lottery or find a pot of gold in a cornfield. They've made savings a lifetime habit—paying themselves first and not wishing that there might be a few dollars left over at the end of the month.

You should be #1 on your payroll.

What does this mean?

If you're like most folks, you sit down once or twice a month and pay all your bills. Then you wonder where all your money went, and why there's none left over for you, and why you don't have any money saved for a rainy day.

To create a legacy for your children or grandchildren, make savings your *top priority*.

Some of you may think this tip is too simple or obvious. However, I have found that some of the most financially sophisticated people with whom I've worked neglect to treat personal savings as a priority. It's never too early or too late to create a lifelong habit of saving money. All of us have long-term goals and dreams—buying our first car, a home, sending children to college, and a comfortable retirement. Those are "big ticket" items!

You work hard for your money. Your savings deserve to be at the top of your list of "bills to pay." So do it! Start with a modest amount for a few weeks or months, writing a check payable to yourself each time you sit down to pay your other bills. Then send your "paycheck" directly to your savings account. Make a note in your checkbook to increase the amount of your "paycheck"—to give yourself a savings raise—after three months and then again after six months.

# Try This Experiment

The next time you withdraw cash from an ATM, take 10% of the amount you've taken out and put it in a separate compartment of your wallet or purse—out of sight, out of mind for the time being. Forget it's there. Then do whatever you'd normally do—go shopping, buy gas for the car, take the kids to the movies.

You'll probably realize that you've managed without having to use the money that you tucked away. Of course, you've had it with you all along in case of an unforeseen emergency.

Next time you take money from the ATM, do the same thing. But this time, take that 10% to the bank and deposit it into your savings account. You'll still have access to it in case of an emergency—but you'll get along pretty well without it being in your wallet or purse.

And bingo! You've started a savings plan!

# Easy Ways to Save

If you have automatic or direct deposit of your paychecks from work, ask your employer or your financial advisor how you can "split" your deposit. Sign the form so that a modest dollar amount or a percentage of each paycheck goes directly into your savings account. If it doesn't ever reach your checking/ATM account, you won't be tempted to spend it. It's already "gone!"

If you have a credit union where you work, you can probably have deposits made directly from your paychecks into your credit union savings account, too.

The key is to regularly, routinely, get the money out of your checking account, out of your paycheck, out of your pocket and into a savings plan. Yes, it's there, and yes, you could get to it if you really needed it…but it's tucked away in savings where it can grow steadily with your regular deposits and compounding interest.

## SIMON SAYS...

Indulge yourself. Treat yourself better. Who deserves to be at the top of the list when you're doling out your hard-earned cash? And who will be very happy to have that nice, fat savings account someday for an important, long-term goal? You, of course.

◆

# SIMON SAYS:
# BE RESPONSIBLE FOR
# YOUR OWN MONEY

◆

SOUNDS LIKE SOMETHING MAMA would say, right? She probably did, in fact—over and over and over. Well, mama was right. She set a good example for you, and you can do the same for your family.

You can only work so many hours in a day, a week, a year, or ten years. You can only be paid what the "going rate" is in your geographic area for the skills, knowledge and experience you have. You won't be paid $100 per hour for a job that typically pays $18, no matter how hard you work or how well you do it. And—bad news— you won't win the lottery.

## A Precious Commodity in Limited Supply

Therefore, the money you earn and have is a very precious commodity in limited supply. So you need to be responsible for it. Save some. Make wise decisions and choices when you spend it to get the most value from every dollar. Take advantage of any and every opportunity to save it and to make it grow. The IRS offers legitimate ways in which you can save money, reduce your taxes, and defer the payment of income taxes. Use those techniques!

If you're not sure how to save it or spend it or take advantage of tax advantages available, don't be afraid to ask for help. You can't be an expert in everything, but you can find an expert—a professional, experienced financial advisor—who spends all of his or her time learning about these financial planning tools and strategies and helping others use them.

## SIMON SAYS...

It won't cost you anything to talk to someone, and the second opinion you get from a seasoned professional may give you exactly the information and direction you need. It's always comforting to get a second opinion about almost anything—from our health to the health of our finances—as long as the second opinion comes from an expert.

◆

# SIMON SAYS: BUILD AN EMERGENCY FUND

◆

YOU'VE GOT A GOOD JOB with a financially sound company. Your spouse has a good job, too. You have a mortgage and monthly bills and you're paying them on time.

What could go wrong with this picture? According to Murphy's Law, almost everything. The opportunity to build your legacy can be wiped out without warning.

If you're living paycheck to paycheck, what will you do when there is a layoff or downsizing where either you or your spouse work? What if a hurricane or tornado rips off your roof next week?

Murphy's Law says that, "If something can go wrong, it will." No doubt about it. There will be a financial emergency in your future—next month, next year, ten years from now. Do you have an emergency fund stashed safely away to take care of that emergency?

## Save for Six Months of Rainy Days

To protect yourself from unexpected financial challenges that can derail your plans to build your financial legacy, you should have a rainy day fund that can cover all of your monthly expenses for at least six months. In addition to an emergency fund, I personally operate with $10,000 in my checking account as a "zero" balance. The question is what amount of saving/liquidity will let you sleep better at night.

It's easy to get started. First, make a list of all of your regular monthly expenses for the past six months. Use your checkbook stubs to help. List:

Mortgage payment _____

Homeowner insurance premium _____

Condominium fees _____

Auto loan payment for all vehicles _____

Auto insurance premiums for all vehicles _____

Health, disability, life insurance premiums _____

Credit card payments _____

Electricity _____

Oil or natural gas for heating _____

Telephone _____

Cable TV, Internet service _____

Trash collection _____

Home maintenance and repair _____

Groceries and household supplies _____

School lunches, books, fees _____

Tuition, room and board _____

Physician and dentist appointments _____

Prescription medications (cost or co-pay) _____

Alimony, child support _____

Any other payments you must make each month _____

Charity _____

Vacation _____

Add up the **total** amount of your monthly expenses: _____

Now multiply it by six.  Total x 6 = _____

Now you know about how much you should have in your emergency fund to protect you for six months.

# Keep Your Fund in a
# Money Market Account

You'll want to have easy access to your emergency dollars.

If you use them to purchase certificates of deposit, you'll pay a penalty fee to cash them in early, before they mature.

Your fund would be very convenient in your checking or savings account—maybe too convenient and easy to "borrow" from on occasion.

I tell my clients to open a money market account for their emergency funds. Most if not all money market accounts come with a checkbook so that you can quickly get cash or make payments from your account. But money market accounts also pay interest! So you'll be earning interest, have immediate access, and you won't be tempted to spend those emergency dollars because they're in a separate account that you don't use regularly.

Of course, we don't know and can't predict when an emergency is going to happen. Maybe you'll never have to touch your emergency fund. That's okay, because it's safely tucked away, earning interest, and it will always be there. You'll sleep better at night, knowing that it's there.

If you do have an emergency, though, what would your other options be to quickly get your hands on a substantial amount of cash? Could you borrow from relatives and friends? Could you sell your jewelry or antique Corvette? Will a bank give you a personal loan if you're not working? Think realistically about where the money you desperately need might come from, and when you might need it.

The reality for most of us is that we have no quick, immediate source for a substantial amount of cash. I'll say again what I've said over and over again to my clients and in this book:

You have to take full responsibility for yourself and your finances.

If you don't have an emergency fund firmly in place, make it your top priority for now to set up one and fund it, using the numbers you arrived at in the exercise above.

Then you'll only have one more thing to do. Re-calculate the monthly numbers about once every two or three years. If you've traded up to a more expensive car, your monthly payments and auto insurance are probably higher. Heating oil costs may have gone up significantly since you first did your calculations.

## SIMON SAYS...

After you've re-calculated, make the additional deposits necessary to be sure your emergency fund is sufficiently funded to truly take care of you and your family—if or when you need it.

◆

# SPENDING

◆

# NOTES

# SIMON SAYS: FOR ONE MONTH, USE ONLY A CREDIT OR DEBIT CARD

◆

DO YOU HAVE A HOLE IN YOUR POCKET? That's the way it seems a lot of the time. You leave the ATM with $100 cash, and before you know it, you're out of cash and headed back to the ATM for more. And if you really concentrate, you can probably remember where about half of the original $100 went. Where did you spend the rest? (By the way, many banking institutions charge an ATM fee, so be sure you know what the costs are to accessing your own money.)

To find out where you spend your money, leave a paper trail.

Here's an interesting experiment. I'll bet you'll find it eye opening—enlightening—and educational.

For one entire month, charge every single purchase you make on your credit or debit card and keep the receipts. (You may want to carry a bit of cash for the vending machines at work or the retail, fast food, and convenience stores that require a minimum purchase of at least $20 before they will accept your credit card. But keep track of that cash, too.) Keep all of your charges on the same card.

If you share a joint account, have your spouse or partner do the same thing.

When your statement from that month arrives in the mail or you view it online, you'll have a pretty comprehensive and accurate record of where your money goes.

Where does the paper trail take you?

It will take you on an interesting journey.

The first place you'll go—if you examine it carefully and critically—is "The Land of Enlightenment." You may discover that you spend at least $150 every time you and your family go out for a "casual" dinner. You may find that you're doing more than just browsing on your Saturday morning trips with your child to the local bookstore; you've been spending $50 or more every Saturday morning on books and magazines! Use the paper trail to become enlightened as to where your money goes every month.

The next place you'll probably go is "The Land of Guilt." Are you staring at all of the charges for fast-food meals you don't even remember having? Are you asking yourself, "Why did I spend all that money at the book store?" Are you wondering, "Did I really use that much gasoline this month?" When you're asking questions like those, you're in "The Land of Guilt"—but just there long enough to get directions to "The Land of Fiscal Responsibility."

Analyzing your paper trail this way will give you some very clear direction and focus as to where your money goes and where you can make positive changes in your spending.

To save money, consider carpooling. Head for the library or the used bookstore on Saturday mornings. Leave your credit card at home when you're headed for the mall; limit yourself to spending only what cash you have in your pocket.

I call it behavioral spending. Identifying your personal expenses and non-essential expenditures is half of the battle to gain control of your finances and begin a serious savings and investment plan. Here's the key to winning that battle, though: Once you start saving money with your newly found awareness, open a savings account or money market account.

Take the money you save each month and stash it away in your new account.

This strategy can be difficult, I know. If you "saved" $100 by not going out to dinner Friday night, does that mean you have the $100 to deposit into your account? Most likely you don't have it because you were going to charge the bill to your credit card.

I tell my clients to do one more thing. You've "saved" that $100. Now go to your ATM and transfer $100 from your checking to your savings account. Now you have truly saved that money.

If you're not sure about this idea, be conservative at first. "Save" the $100, but only move half of that amount into your savings account.

## SIMON SAYS...

When you start getting statements about your growing savings account—your new paper trail—you'll know you are really on to something good and that it's working! Your savings plan will set a good example for your family and help you build your legacy.

◆

# SIMON SAYS:
# USE VIP OR "SPECIAL CUSTOMER" CARDS

◆

BUILDING YOUR LEGACY and teaching your children how to be financially responsible is not just a matter of setting aside money by *saving more*; it's also a matter of *spending less*. Here's one simple strategy that you and your kids can use every day.

In the competitive world of retailing, stores want to capture and keep your business so that you'll become a loyal customer. To do that, most supermarket chains and a growing number of other types of stores are now offering "customer cards" or "VIP cards" that give users a special discount on featured items.

Some retailers use the cards to offer "clipless coupons." You no longer need to clip and carry around a big pile of coupons when you go shopping; if you have the store's special customer card, you'll get the advertised coupon price.

I've heard some people say that they don't want those customer cards because, in order to get one, they have to provide personal information and identification—name, address, and phone number. They're also concerned that the stores will use their information and compile data

I understand the concern for privacy these days; it seems like more and more businesses are collecting information about us and our personal buying habits. But I'm not convinced that they're hurting us as individuals by collecting this data. Some grocery stores run special promotions for their cardholders, too; one chain gives a free Thanksgiving turkey to cardholders who spend at least $300 in their stores during the months of October and November. They track the total purchases by computer.

My suggestion, then, is to apply for these customer cards wherever you shop, even if you don't shop in some of them regularly. Buy an inexpensive credit card case to organize all of your shopping cards. Many stores also offer mini-cards that you can put on your car key ring. Then use them all the time!

## SIMON SAYS...

Remember that it's not only saving when you buy that matters; it's also important to put your savings to good use. I'll repeat here what I said in the tip about shopping at discount stores: don't fritter away your savings! If you saved $15 on groceries this week by using your card, put $10 of it into a savings account. I know I'm using small dollar amounts as examples but if you can get into the discipline of being conscious of saving money these dollars will add up and you'll be saving for your retirement, for a vacation home, or for your child's college education.

◆

# SIMON SAYS: SHOP AT DISCOUNT STORES

◆

THIRTY YEARS AGO, the name "discount store" conjured up an image of a retail store selling damaged, seconds, or close-out merchandise. Prices were good but you had to settle for whatever brand the store happened to have in stock on the day you were shopping. And you had to check carefully for defects.

Today's discount stores are something else entirely. Retail stores like Target, Sam's Club and Wal-Mart offer a wide selection of top quality merchandise and brand names. You'll save substantial dollars buying the same brands as you'll find in the more expensive stores, boutiques, and malls.

They're able to offer big savings because they buy directly from the manufacturers in enormous quantities—truckloads of toasters and air conditioners and shampoo—and pay lower prices. They can afford to earn a few cents or a few dollars less on each item they sell to you because they're selling in such large volume. They have lower overhead than the mall stores.

## "Discount" Means "Convenience"

Another huge advantage to these giant retailers is the availability of almost everything you need under one roof. You no longer have to go to the garden store for grass seed, the hardware store for paint, the toy store for a child's birthday gift, the greeting card shop for wrapping paper, and the pet shop for dog food.

With one list, you'll find yourself saving time and money with one-stop shopping. You'll save gasoline and wear and tear on your vehicle. You'll reduce your stress level, and have more time to spend on things you enjoy doing—and spend time with your family.

Efficiency is the name of the game, and these superstores offer you an opportunity to be super-efficient with your time and your money. Put a schedule in place to go to these stores once every month and stock up on the things that you and your family buy and use all the time. You'll save the last-minute "we're out of toothpaste" running around that is expensive.

Know your prices, however. Buying in bulk can be a bargain, but it's not always the case. Learn how to read the unit pricing tags so that you can compare a regular size bottle of laundry detergent with a "super" size one. Also, keep in mind that when you buy in bulk, you'll be toting heavy bags and boxes around, possibly hurting your back, and you'll need to store those items for a while until you use them.

Here's the most important idea of saving money by shopping at the discount superstores.

Let's say you've saved money. You expected to pay $200 for a new vacuum cleaner but found it on sale for $150. You've saved $50.

## Simon Says...

Don't fritter away your savings! Take the $50 you've saved—or even $30 of it—and put it into that savings account for retirement or funding your child's college expenses. Do that regularly, and you'll see your account begin to grow steadily. It hasn't really cost you anything to start and grow this account because you're using money that you had planned and expected to spend anyway.

Now you've got a head start on long-term savings for important goals like your child's education or your own retirement!

◆

# MAKING YOUR MONEY GROW

◆

# NOTES

# SIMON SAYS: UNDERSTAND COMPOUND INTEREST

◆

"LITTLE OLD LADY LEAVES $2 MILLION TO HER CATS!" You've undoubtedly seen stories like this in the newspaper—the elderly librarian or the maintenance worker at City Hall who has amassed a substantial nest egg despite the fact that they were "middle income" people.

Did you wonder, "How did they do that? How did they accumulate millions on their income?"

Of course there is always the possibility that the individual inherited a bundle of money from someone else, or perhaps he or she won the lottery twenty years ago.

In most cases, however, I'd bet that their secret was saving wisely—another benefit of compound interest.

## The "Eighth Wonder of the World"

You may have learned about compound interest when you were in grade school; it was always a popular subject for "word problems" on math tests and, as a concept, it was pretty dull.

Today, though, you should see compounding as an incredibly powerful tool for the almost painless accumulation of wealth. It's "the eighth wonder of the world," say some financial planners with only slight exaggeration.

Here is an example to show you the "magic" of compounding. We'll assume you start at age twenty putting $20 a week into a savings account. The goal is to have a nice nest egg when you retire at age seventy. We know that interest rates being paid on savings accounts are ridiculously low right now, and will vary all over the place during a fifty-year time span, so we'll use an historical average of 4% per year. (Figures below are rounded to the nearest dollar.)

At the end of the first year of savings, you'll have $1,040 plus interest—or $1,050.

At the end of five years, you'll have $5,478 in your account.

At the end of ten years, you'll have $11,558 in your account.

At the end of twenty years, you'll have $25,788.

At the end of thirty years, you'll have a total of $43,307.

At the end of forty years, you'll have $64,876.

## SIMON SAYS...

**Finally, when you're ready to retire at age seventy, and after following this strategy faithfully for fifty years, you'll have a total nest egg of $91,431. The amazing thing is that you will have deposited only $52,000 of your own money. All the rest is interest you have earned!**

Don't believe me? You can figure it out yourself. Just Google "compound interest calculator" and you'll see a bunch of free websites that offer calculators. Just plug in the numbers and see the results. (Use different interest rates and see the difference in the values. Remember the higher the interest rate, the more risk and volatility you will experience.)

## But You're Not Twenty Any More!

It is true that the longer you make deposits to your savings account and the longer it earns interest, the more money you'll have for your retirement nest egg. But you can compensate. When the length of time is shorter, you'll have to make your weekly deposits larger to catch up.

Let's say that you're forty years old, so we'll assume you only have thirty years to build your nest egg to return at 70. Let's use a 4% annual rate, compounded quarterly and put $50 a week into your savings account. Let's see how the numbers come out with these assumptions:

At the end of the first year, you'll have $2,600 plus interest—or $2,626.

At the end of ten years, you'll have $28,895 in your account.

At the end of twenty years, you'll have $64,470.

At the end of thirty years, when you're seventy, you'll have $108,268.

$78,000 of that is the money you've deposited. The rest is all interest you've earned.

There's yet another strategy to make your nest egg bigger. Make an initial commitment to put in $2,600 ($50 a week) every year. Then when you get a raise, bonus, or a refund check from the IRS, make a commitment to put that "found" money into your savings account as well.

You can see how compounding can magically turn a little nest egg into a larger one, and you can see that it's almost painless because the weekly savings amounts can be relatively small as long as they are made regularly.

This is called "paying yourself first."

Here's even better news. Throughout this tip we've been talking about "plain old vanilla" savings accounts—which typically pay the lowest interest of any financial investment. Look instead at the interest rates your bank or credit union is paying for certificates of deposit—especially for the five-year and even ten year CDs. The interest is higher than what you'll earn on the passbook savings plan.

Now let's look at the average annual return on a mutual fund or even an individual stock. Be sure to look at the long-term numbers, because the stock market—like savings bank interests rates—goes up and down over the short term, and your money will be invested for a long time.

You'll most likely find a number of mutual funds that, over five or ten year spans, have averaged returns of 5% or 8%, and some even as high as 10% annually. Once you find one paying a higher interest rate than the 4% we've used in our example above, go to the Internet and do your search for "compound interest calculator." Then plug into the calculator a lot of different numbers—differing amounts you will put in each year, the various interest rates you've found, how often interest is compounded and how many years you plan to follow this investment strategy.

The numbers will amaze and delight you, I guarantee! You'll really see and appreciate the power and magic of compound interest.

Remember that the money in your savings account and in certificates of deposit is insured by the Federal Deposit Insurance Company (FDIC) for up to $250,000 per depositor. The money you invest in stocks, bonds, and mutual funds is *not* insured by the FDIC and it's not insured by the companies issuing the stock or the managers of the mutual funds. Depending on the swings of the market, you may end up losing money, as many investors did during the Great Recession that began in 2008.

The good news is that the up and down swings of the stock market tend to even out over time and even out in the "plus" column. Over the past fifty years the Dow Jones Industrial Average has risen from about 1,000 to about 15,000—a hefty 1,500% increase! That's why I always emphasize the long-term approach when I talk to my clients about financial planning and investment strategies.

## SIMON SAYS...

I urge you to take full advantage of the power of compounding. Open that savings account today or other long term investment and keep making weekly deposits. Then use an online calculator to see how the "magic" of compounding will pay off handsomely in the future.

◆

# SIMON SAYS:
# SET UP A 529 COLLEGE SAVINGS PLAN

◆

FOR MANY OF OUR PARENTS and grandparents, the dream of attending college was just that—a dream. Today it's pretty much a necessity for our children to ensure that they'll have the education they'll need to succeed and compete in the world of work. A college education is one of the true, lasting gifts we can give to our children.

## How Much Money Will You Need?

How old are your children? How many years until they'll be ready for college? When they're ready to go, will you have enough money in savings to pay each child's tuition, room, board, books, clothing, and other expenses for four years?

Use a college work sheet to estimate how much those things will cost when your child is ready to go to college.

Even if you don't yet have children, you could set up a 529 College Savings Plan right away. Many of my retired clients are going back to school and are taking classes in retirement. You too can fund your tuition and the money is growing tax free while in accumulation. (Check with your CPA or accountant to determine the tax benefits in the state in which you live, such as in New York where you contribute money to the New York state-sponsored plan.) (You Receive a deduction up to 10k on your NY State Tax Return.) It's called a 529 Plan because it's named after the section of the IRS Tax Code.

Let's say your daughter is now five years old. You open a 529 Plan for her college education, and faithfully make monthly deposits of $100 to the plan. All of your deposits are invested inside mutual funds, growing tax-deferred until it is withdrawn. (Remember that if the funds are used to pay for higher education, then there are no federal taxes due. If the funds are not used for qualified educational expenses, federal taxes must be paid on the earnings plus a 10% penalty for withdrawal.) By the time your daughter turns 18 years old, you will have deposited $15,600. Assuming a modest 4% rate of return on the mutual funds for that period of time, you will now have $16,094 in the 529 Savings Plan for her college education.

There are some extra benefits as well.

♦ Money withdrawn is income tax free as long as it is spent for education, according to the specific terms of the Plan you're using.

♦ You continue to retain control of the account at all times so that your child may only spend it for educational purposes until she reaches the age of thirty. She can't take it and buy a red convertible, as she would be able to do if you had created a UGMA, UTMA, or custodial account for her.

♦ If your daughter chooses not to go to college, you can change the name of the beneficiary from her to another person without penalty.

♦ You can change your 529 Plan Account investment choices once a year.

♦ Your Social Security number is used on the 529 Plan Account rather than your child's. When the college financial aid officer asks how much money your child has available to pay for his or her college, he or she only considers 5.6% of the money in your 529 Account to be available assets for the purpose of calculating financial need.

It's essential to remember that your dollars will be in the 529 Account for a period of years. Remember, too, that there is a financial penalty for withdrawing the money for any purpose other than education.

The other caution is that the funds are invested in mutual funds. These types of investments are not insured or guaranteed, and therefore it's possible that your 529 Plan may lose account value, depending on the type of account you choose.

## SIMON SAYS...

529 Plans continue to grow in popularity as parents begin to realize what the cost of college may be in ten or fifteen years, and because of the tax benefits as well. Today, there are many 529 Plan sponsors to choose from. 529 Plan funds can be used for tuition and expenses at trade schools as well as for college.

Talk to your financial advisor, who has expertise in 529 Plans and who has more than one Plan sponsor from which to choose. Ask what other methods of saving for college you should also consider for you and your family, so you can make an informed decision.

◆

# SIMON SAYS:
# OPEN A SMALL-DEPOSIT
# MUTUAL FUND ACCOUNT

◆

A MUTUAL FUND IS A TYPE of professionally managed investment product that pools money from many investors to purchase securities. While there is no legal definition of mutual fund, in the United States the term is most commonly applied only to those collective investment strategies that are available to the general public, registered with the Securities and Exchange Commission (SEC), and open-ended in nature.

It's often been said that, for the small investor—or a new investor—mutual funds may be the safest, easiest way to invest in the stock market. Rather than buying the shares of one company, you're investing in a fund that pools your money with many other investors and then uses it to buy shares of many companies. This pooled approach diversifies your risk. In addition, the fund has professional investors managing it, deciding what stocks to buy and sell and when.

There are many types of mutual funds, differentiated by how the money is invested and how the fund is managed. You can choose a fund that focuses on one type of investment, such as bonds, stocks, international, small cap, large cap etc. You can choose a fund that has many specific characteristics that appeal to your risk tolerance and the goals of your money, such as growth and income.

These investments entail risk and you need time to understand both the positives and negatives before you invest your money. Please remember what Simon Says: "It's your money and you need to be responsible for it."

# Choosing the Right Fund for You

With all of the choices out there, how do you know which to choose when you're first beginning to invest in mutual funds? You can look at the fund's prospectus or read it (How Exciting)—a written document explaining its investment goals, listing the companies in which it invests, and showing its track record—and track how it has performed over various periods of time.

This is the sort of basic investment education that you can share with your children from a young age. You can show them some of the assets in the fund, and follow its performance over weeks and months.

Mutual funds can be a relatively safe, long-term investment haven for new investors, but they may or may not be the right choice for you. Talk to your financial advisor. He or she will know which type of fund is a good fit based on your investment goals and risk tolerance, and will be able to recommend one that matches your needs.

If the right investment vehicle turns out to be mutual funds, your advisor will help you find one that allows a relatively small amount of money to open an account and relatively small deposit amounts— perhaps $25 or $50 at a time.

This is important because some funds require thousands of dollars to open an account, and require deposits thereafter of at least $1,000. Now, you may have a lot of money to open your account with— perhaps from an inheritance, lottery winning, or a year-end bonus at work—but how often will you have $1,000 in a lump sum to deposit into your account? And if you do have that much extra cash, what are the chances that you'll actually deposit it in your mutual fund account?

## SIMON SAYS...

It's my experience that, if the dollar amounts are affordable, you're more likely to keep putting money into your mutual fund account.

You'll find that, when you get into the habit of making regular deposits (remember "Simon Says: Pay Yourself First"), you'll see your account grow, and that will in turn encourage you to deposit even more money. If you have young children you may even want to informally assign a portion of your investment to them, so they can follow along and see how their shares grow. Remember that the investment value will fluctuate and shares when redeemed may be worth more or less than their original cost.

◆

# SIMON SAYS: JOIN YOUR COMPANY'S 401(K) RETIREMENT PLAN

◆

IF YOUR COMPANY OFFERS a 401(k) retirement plan and the company matches some of your contributions and you're not a member, you're missing out on free money!

The 401(k) retirement plan is named after the section of the Internal Revenue Code—Section 401(k)—that authorizes this unique incentive for you to save toward retirement.

For university, civil government, and not-for-profit employees there's the 403(b) plan, which has similar characteristics and benefits to a 401(k).

Many employers offer 401(k) plans for their eligible employees. Note the word "offer." Participating in these plans is voluntary. You don't have to participate if you don't want to, but there are several good reasons why you should want to enroll immediately if you haven't already—and if you meet your company plan's eligibility requirements.

1.  You save money toward a long-term goal like retirement. Earlier in the book I talked about "paying yourself first." This is another painless way to do that. You can contribute a percentage of your pay—before any taxes are withheld—to your 401(k) account. Presto! The money is stashed away in your plan account, so you're not tempted to spend it. In fact, you'll pay some hefty penalties for withdrawing it unless you meet some very rigid requirements.

2.  Many employers contribute matching dollars to their employees' 401(k) plans. That's free money to you! They're not required to do it, but many do because it's a nice fringe benefit for their people.

The match can be any percentage, but many companies offer 50% matching. That means that for every dollar you put into your account, your company will contribute another fifty cents. These plans typically have limits on matching; that means that an employer may match only the first 3% of your pay that you contribute.

If your company matches your contribution at any percentage, that's *free money* to you. (Yes, I know I'm repeating myself.) So your 401(k) account grows by the dollars you put in and also by the dollars that your company puts in. It's a good deal!

3.  You get income tax benefits. With every paycheck your money goes into your account before any taxes are taken out of it, so you'll pay less in income taxes while you're working and contributing. But you'll have to pay the income tax on that money when you take it out of your account at retirement. The good news is that, for most people, their tax rate at retirement is lower than it was while they worked. So you'll probably pay less in income taxes than you would otherwise have paid if you were working.

Remember that the funds in your 401(k) don't just sit in a savings account in a bank. The funds are typically pooled and invested, like a mutual fund. 401(k) plan investment options are managed by professional money managers; some are well known in the financial industry. You may be able to choose how the dollars in your account are invested—perhaps in a variety of different types of mutual funds, money market funds, bonds, company stock, or other types of investments. Those investments can earn dividends and interest, increasing the values of your contribution—and of course, on the money that the company contributed to your account as well. Take note that it is also possible that you'll lose some of your money if the stock market goes down, because the dollars in your 401(k) account are not insured against loss, so there is some risk. So if you can control the investment options, choose those that reflect your risk/reward tolerance. If you can diversify among several options, that's usually a safer route than putting everything into one type of fund or into your company's stock, for example.

Please note that your employer's stock should never represent more than 10% of the total value of your 401(k). You want to diversify and generally do not want to have all of your eggs in one basket.

# Here's an Example of How Your 401(k) Plan Works

Let's say that your annual income is $50,000. You contribute 10% of that amount, or $5,000, to your 401(k) account. When income tax time rolls around, you'll only have to pay tax on $45,000 because the $5,000 you put into your 401(k) is excluded from your income. It will grow on a tax-deferred basis in your plan. You won't have to pay any income taxes on it until you take it out.

Now let's say that you earn $50,000 and put $5,000 of it away into your 401(k) plan, but your employer matches your contributions dollar for dollar up to 3% of your income. Your 401(k) account will have your $5,000 plus the company's matching contribution—the free money—of $1,500. Now you have $6,500 growing long-term in your account. ★★★★★(3% contribution is based on your income of $50,000)

To open your 401(k) account, visit or call the human resources office and ask about the enrollment process and for a brochure about the plan. The person you talk with will tell you if you're eligible to enroll, depending on how long you've been with the company and how many hours per week you work.

If you're eligible, you'll have some forms to fill out to open your 401(k) account and to allow the company to make automatic withdrawals from your pay and deposit the money in your account. Though your plan offers investment options, you'll be asked to select what percentage of your contributions you want to go into the various choices offered. Your choices aren't "carved in stone," however. You'll have the opportunity to change your choices several times each year, depending on how your company's plan is set up. You'll also receive quarterly or annual statements with complete details about your 401(k) account.

# 401(k) Fees

Another thing to keep in mind is that there are fees associated with the management of your 401(k) plan. Read and understand the fees that the plan providers charge. Some charges may not be obvious because they are built into the fund's expenses.

Over the years, consumers complained that it was difficult to figure out what criteria the fees were based on and how much they were. In 2012, new rules from the U.S. Department of Labor were designed to increase the transparency of 401(k) fees. One of the requirements was a new format for quarterly statements that clearly shows all the fees. The new statement format includes a table showing all fees and the actual returns for each investment before fees are taken out.

Employers have a responsibility too. Under the new rules, employers are required to determine whether fees being charged are reasonable in relation to the national market, and whether lower fees are available for the same services. While the rules call for heavy fines for employers who fail to comply, not all employers may be up to speed, and it's worthwhile for you to inquire with your human resources department to make sure they are aware of the rules and are in compliance.

# Fund It and Take It With You

If you're not making maximum allowable contributions—or if you're not sure what the maximum is—it's time to visit your human resources department and get some answers.

That's because the maximum allowable amount increases by law each year. Also, there are special provisions for employees ages fifty and over.

The 401(k) plan is not an employee benefit that you just "sign up for" and forget about. It has the potential of growing sheltered from income taxes to a huge amount of money for your retirement. It's also portable, so that if you leave your employer, you can take it with you. If you do move your 401(k), pay very close attention to the requirements, the restrictions, the deadlines, and the penalties for doing so properly. They are not difficult to follow, but if you ignore them or make a mistake or miss a deadline, you can lose big time.

Increase your contributions every chance you get.

◆ You get a pay raise—increase the amount you put into your account.

◆ You get a bonus—increase the amount you put into your account.

◆ Your spouse gets a job or a raise so your family has more disposable income—you can afford to increase your weekly contribution amount. Do it!

◆ A car payment has come to the end of its term and you now have freed up that monthly expense.

Today—*right now*—is the time to increase the amount you put into your 401k plan. Please do this before the monies are reallocated and you look back and say, where did that money go? The word "disposable" above is so important because that's what most of us tend to do—we dispose of any extra money we have or receive rather than save it. Most of the time, we can't even remember how we spent it. But even though the events above may only mean a few dollars more in your pocket each week, those dollars can make a huge difference twenty or thirty years from now if you've safely stashed them away in your 401(k) or 403(b) plan, where they will grow and be invested tax-deferred until retirement.

Simon says that these long-term retirement savings plans are "win, win, win" for you. Even if you're young and not thinking yet about retiring, participating in your company's 401(k) is a great way to save, to receive matching dollars if your company offers that feature, to put off paying income taxes on some of your earnings for many years, and to invest in the market. The sooner you join, the longer you have to collect matching company dollars and possibly earn dividends and interest.

It's essential to remember, however, that these plans are for long-term savings. Don't contribute more than you can afford, because you'll pay taxes and penalties if you need to take money out of your account; in fact, you may lose half of your asset value due to the penalties and taxes. So start with a modest amount. You can increase it later.

Your human resources people can't offer you investment advice, so you'll have to think about the investment choices and make your own decisions. A professional financial planner is a good, objective source of information and can offer recommendations, especially after you've been in the plan for a few years and your 401(k) account really starts to grow.

## SIMON SAYS...

One final reminder: When you get a pay raise or when a car payment has come to the end of its term, don't fritter it away. As soon as your paycheck goes up to the new weekly amount, increase your 401(k) contribution by that many dollars per week. Pretend you never got those extra dollars, and put them away where they can provide you with a significant accumulation of cash down the road. If you don't find a safe place to put these extra dollars, you'll spend them and forget about them.

◆

# SIMON SAYS:
# AVOID TAKING A LOAN FROM YOUR 401(K) OR PROFIT-SHARING ACCOUNT

◆

EACH TIME YOU RECEIVE your 401(k) or profit sharing account statement, when you look at your account balance you might say to yourself, "What harm could there be in taking out a small loan?"

Although there are usually restrictions on withdrawing money from profit sharing and 401(k) accounts, you may find a provision in your company's plan that allows you to take a loan from your account. In fact, according to data from the Employee Benefit Research Institute, nearly 20% of 401(k) plan participants who are eligible to take loans against their retirement savings take advantage of this option.

When you take a loan from your 401(k) or profit sharing account, you are really borrowing money from yourself and from your long-term savings. When you pay it back, you're paying yourself back and you're paying yourself the interest.

What could be wrong with that?

## SIMON SAYS...
"Don't do it!" There are plenty of reasons why it's a bad idea.

First of all, you may lose interest income. You'll recall that 401(k) and profit sharing plans are tax-deferred plans for long-term savings and growth. Suppose you borrow cash from your 401(k) account and agree to pay 6% interest. You'll be paying yourself back your own money and the 6% interest on the loan.

But what if your 401(k) account has been earning ten percent return? The money you borrowed wasn't there earning 10%, so you would be missing out on four percent return. In the investment world we call that the "opportunity cost." It's the cost to you of missing an opportunity to earn money.

◆

# Tax Issues

Another potential problem is if your loan is still outstanding when you leave the company, it creates a taxable event. If you're under age 59-1/2, the IRS will impose a 10% penalty *and* you have to repay the full amount of the loan within sixty days. This could be disastrous, especially if you are leaving your job and you have a gap in income. The Internal Revenue Code has set strict guidelines, rules, and established penalties for 401(k) plan accounts. You need to know all of those provisions before you make a withdrawal or take a loan from one of these accounts to avoid unnecessary penalties.

There are other tax implications. The contributions you make to your 401(k) are in *pretax* dollars. But when you take out a loan, you'll be paying yourself back in *after-tax* dollars. Since taxes are withheld from your salary, you'll need more than the loan amount to pay it back, which can be a significant hidden cost.

If your company's 401(k) or profit sharing plan offers a provision for taking loans, then, of course you can consider borrowing from yourself if you have an urgent need, such as buying your first home or money to pay for health care. But you need to seriously consider the opportunity cost of growing your money—the money you'll want to have later in life for retirement or some other long-term goal—tax deferred.

# It's a Red Flag

Your retirement account should be sacrosanct. It should exist outside your normal operating expenses, and your household budget should be balanced after you factor in your 401(k) contributions. So if you are looking to your 401(k) as a source of funds, Simon says "Stop" and review your household budget. You need to be saving elsewhere—even in a regular plain vanilla savings account—to fund elective expenses such as vacations and home improvements.

Before you consider a loan from your 401(k), look around to see what other sources of money you have so that you don't have to touch your tax deferred nest egg. See if you have any after-tax dollars in your 401(k) account. If the dollars have already been taxed, they are available with no tax penalties. If you own your own home, you may have some additional equity available to borrow against, which you may be able to access through a home equity line of credit. The interest on home equity loans is tax deductible, too.

If you are considering a loan to help your child in college, think twice. Most federal student loans are low interest and students have years to pay them back. You will save money if you can find additional federal student loans.

For a real emergency, you might have to withdraw money from your 401(k) or profit-sharing account. But it's never a good idea to borrow money from yourself and from your own long-term savings for retirement. By doing so, you may be unnecessarily diminishing your financial legacy.

Consider the man who took a 401k loan and then had to leave his job. He faced the unpleasant choice of being forced to repay the loan immediately or take a 10% penalty and have the income be included in his taxable income.

## SIMON SAYS...

You need to pay yourself first. You cannot borrow money for retirement, and Simon Says it's extremely important to have your child or grandchild take some responsibility for the cost of their education.

◆

# SIMON SAYS: CONTRIBUTE THE MAXIMUM TO YOUR 401(K) OR 403(B) PLAN

◆

YOU ENROLLED IN YOUR COMPANY'S retirement savings plan for some good reasons that I outlined in an earlier chapter, most notably to increase your financial legacy. Now that your plan is in place, Simon says to ask yourself this: Am I contributing the maximum amount the plan allows?

Why is this important? If you're not making maximum allowable contributions—or if you're not sure what the maximum is—it's time to visit your human resources department for face-to-face communication or go to the internet for answers. That's because the maximum allowable amount increases by law each year. Also, there are special provisions for older employees—ages 50 and over. The bottom line is that by not contributing the maximum, you could be leaving money on the table.

The 401(k) plan is not an employee benefit that you just sign up for and forget about. It has the potential of growing sheltered from income taxes. It's also portable, so that if you leave your employer, you can take it with you. (If you do move your 401(k), pay very close attention to the requirements, the restrictions, the deadlines, and the penalties for doing so properly. They are not difficult to follow but if you ignore them or make a mistake, there can be significant tax consequences.)

## Increase Your Contributions Every Chance You Get!

You get a pay raise—increase the amount you put into your account.
You get a bonus—increase the amount you put into your account.

Your spouse gets a job or a raise—increase the amount you put into your account.

You start bringing your lunch to work instead of buying lunch out every day—well, you know the answer. Increase the amount you put into your account.

Your car loan payments come to an end—increase the amount you put into your account.

Most of us tend to *spend* any extra money we have or receive rather than *save* it. Most of the time, we can't even remember how we spent it. But even though the events above may only mean a few dollars more in your pocket each week, those dollars can make a huge difference twenty or thirty years from now if you've safely stashed them away in your 401(k) or 403(b) plan, where they will grow tax-deferred until you reach age 59-1/2.

Perhaps when you joined your company's 401(k) plan a few years ago, you weren't sure how much you could afford to contribute from each paycheck, so you chose a modest amount. Look at your plan and your contributions again. Do this at least once a year. Increase the amount you're contributing to the maximum allowed. Review how the investments are allocated. See what the special provisions are for older employees if you're age 50 or older.

In my practice I've worked with clients who have participated in their employers' 401(k) plans for twenty or thirty years. With company matching, regular contributions, and good investment choices, some of my clients have accounts worth hundreds of thousands and even millions of dollars—amounts they never could have saved on their own.

There's another advantage to making regular contributions to your account. You're using a method of investing called "dollar cost averaging." Your money is invested at regular intervals in the same investment. Because you invest the same amount each time, you automatically buy less of the investment when its price is higher and more when its price is lower. Though the method doesn't guarantee a profit or guard against loss in declining markets, the average cost of each share is usually lower than if you buy at random times or if you might try to "time the market," as some investors try to do. For dollar cost averaging to work, you must continue to invest regularly.

## SIMON SAYS...

That's why I say that these plans are "A win, win, win"—and you win the most when you contribute the most. You can't lose when you're receiving "free money" from your employer and "free money" from Uncle Sam, in that you don't have to pay taxes on any of the money until you begin withdrawing it from your account.

Before you do anything with the money in your 401(k)—such as move it to another employer—talk to a professional financial planner. He or she may be able to show you some options and will certainly help you with the paperwork to be sure you meet all of the regulations and deadlines.

◆

# SIMON SAYS:
# OPEN A ROTH IRA

◆

THE DEBATE CONTINUES as to whether or not the Social Security system in our country will be solvent or even exist ten or twenty years from now. I doubt seriously that our elected representatives would ever allow it to disappear.

The reality, however, is that the monthly Social Security checks you'll receive will not be enough for you to comfortably live on. You need to start saving right now to supplement any Social Security benefits you may receive in the future. The tax benefits are certainly an added incentive for you to open an IRA, but even if you're not eligible for the tax benefits, you need to have a regular, methodical system for long-term savings.

If you are self employed or otherwise not eligible to participate in your employer's retirement savings plan—such as a profit-sharing, 401(k) or 403(b) plan—then it's up to you to set up and fund your own retirement savings plan. You can't rely solely on Social Security to meet all of your financial needs after retirement, and you need to build your financial legacy.

One answer is to open an individual retirement account, or IRA.

To encourage Americans to save money for their own retirement, individual retirement accounts were first introduced in 1974 with the enactment of the Employee Retirement Income Security Act (ERISA), and since then the concept has been modified several times.

Basically, an IRA is a special long-term savings account that may have some tax advantages based on your annual income. There are several varieties, but we'll focus on traditional IRAs and Roth IRAs.

As of this writing if you are not eligible to participate in a company sponsored retirement plan, you can each contribute up to $5,500 to an individual retirement account. Your contributions are deducted from your income for the year in which you make them; in other words, you don't pay any income taxes on the amount you contribute. So your IRA contributions become a deductible expense when you're preparing your income tax returns.

If you are over age fifty, the regulations have recently been enhanced so that you may contribute up to $6,500 per year.

If you earn more than the allowable amount (which may change from year to year) and you are a participant in a retirement plan, you can still make contributions to your IRA, but you may not be allowed to deduct your contributions from your gross income. In other words, the dollars you set aside in your IRA are *after-tax* dollars.

## Opportunities for Investing

Depending on how you set up your IRA account, you may have some investment choices. For example, you can establish your IRA with an investment or brokerage firm and use your IRA dollars to invest in mutual funds or individual stocks. Any dividends you earn stay in your IRA account, and income taxes on those earnings are deferred until you take the money out of the account. You could also deposit your IRA contributions in a regular bank savings account.

Regardless of how you invest your IRA dollars, your contributions, dividends, interest, and earnings continue to grow. Income taxes on the earnings are deferred, so you don't have to pay them until you withdraw money from your IRA account.

There's a catch. Because the IRA is intended to be a retirement savings account, you cannot withdraw any money from your account until you are age 59-1/2. If you do withdraw some or all of it, you will be required to pay 10% of the money to the IRS as a penalty for early withdrawal, plus income taxes.

Furthermore, when you reach age 70-1/2, you are required by

the IRS to begin taking mandatory withdrawals, or required minimum distribution (RMD).

# Roth IRA vs. Traditional IRA

Now that you've learned about individual retirement accounts—what they are, who is eligible to have them, and the potential tax advantages you may gain through your IRA account—I'm going to talk you out of owning a traditional IRA. Simon says consider opening a Roth IRA instead—or, if you already have a regular IRA, you may want to convert it to a Roth IRA. Speak with your financial or tax advisor to determine if a conversion is suitable for you.

The Roth IRA was established by the Taxpayer Relief Act of 1997 and named for its chief legislative sponsor, Senator William Roth of Delaware. The Roth IRA offers potentially significant advantages from the traditional IRA.

Always check with your CPA for a specific understanding of your tax situation. In general, with a regular IRA your contributions may be tax-deductible. With a Roth IRA, all of your contributions are made with *after-tax* dollars. You've already paid the income tax on that money. As with a regular IRA, you can set it up to invest in mutual funds, stocks, bonds, or other investments.

In addition, your distributions from your Roth IRA at age 59-1/2 is income tax free. Another benefit is that you are not required to take withdrawals from it, as you are with a regular IRA at 70-1/2. When you die, your Roth IRA passes to your spouse income tax free. When he or she dies, it can then be passed along to your children income tax free.

When you close out the regular IRA, you'll have to pay income taxes on the money you take out. The money you then put into the Roth IRA earns dividends and interest that are income tax free to you when you take it out, or to your spouse or heirs after you die.

If you or your spouse participates in any type of profit-sharing or 401(k) plan through your employer, you may not be eligible for the tax deduction feature of an IRA. Many people think this is unfair. A client recently mentioned that she can't have a tax-deductible IRA because her husband earns too much money and contributes to his 401(k) at work. Fortunately, there is a solution—the Roth IRA.

The Roth IRA is an extraordinary savings tool, and depending on your future tax bracket may be better than a regular IRA because there are no income taxes due on any distributions.

With the regular IRA, you may be eligible for some tax benefit on the dollars you deposit into it initially, but as it grows and earns interest and dividends over many years, the tax due when you withdraw the money may be significantly *more* than the tax saving you enjoyed at the beginning. With the Roth, there are no income taxes to pay at the end, no matter how large the account value has grown. Many people feel we may be paying higher taxes in the future, so it really depends on your specific circumstances.

More importantly, if you have accumulated a significant estate, you can name several beneficiaries and each gets to elect how he or she wants to distribute the assets in the Roth IRA. Your son may take the money—tax-free—while your daughter may choose to leave her share in the Roth IRA, where it can continue to grow without income taxes for her lifetime. She will be required to take a RMD out annually to satisfy the IRA rules. If your estate is large enough, it may make sense to convert your IRA to a Roth IRA with the understanding that the income taxes paid is reducing your taxable estate/net worth (In essence if the estate tax is 50% and you just paid the income taxes, the government just paid half of the income tax to allow you to place this money into a tax free vehicle to accumulate for your children and loved ones in the Roth).

Elsewhere in this book I discuss converting the assets in your 401(k) or 403(b) plan into an IRA and then into a Roth IRA. Currently the law says that we need to take that middle step of "transferring" your assets first into a regular IRA and then converting that into a Roth IRA.

## SIMON SAYS...

Moving assets from a 401(k) to create an IRA and then a Roth IRA is a strategy that I recommend to some of my clients because there are so many advantages for long term financial planning. Talk to your financial advisor and tax advisor about the best course of action for you to take, based on your unique situation.

Remember, if you do not qualify to take an IRA deduction and you have the disposable income to save from retirement, Simon says establish an IRA and immediately convert it to a Roth. Talk to your tax advisor to determine how this would relate to your situation.

◆

# PLANNING
# AHEAD

◆

# NOTES

# SIMON SAYS:
# ARE YOU A SAVER OR A SPENDER?

◆

THERE'S AN OLD SAYING, "If you think money can't buy happiness, you're obviously shopping in the wrong place."

When you're ready to make long-range financial plans, it's worthwhile to step back for a moment and think about what money really means to you. Is it a piece of paper to exchange with a merchant for something to make you happy? Is it a sign of security—the more money you have, the more secure you will feel? Is it like play money on a board game—it's fun to collect it and see if you can get more than all the other players?

For most of us, money isn't just money. It's a symbol. It stands for some value, some belief, something other than a piece of paper or a little plastic card. How you think about money says a lot about you—your upbringing, your competitive nature, your need for security, your need for admiring groupies who want to share your wealth.

But there's a more important question than what does money mean to you?

## Are You a Saver or a Spender?

If you're a saver, you know that, at the end of the month, you can most likely pay your bills. You may not have the best clothes, the flashiest car, the mansion on the hill, but you have no debts other than perhaps a mortgage and a car payment. You have a nest egg that provides you and your family with financial security.

If you're a spender, you know that, at the of the month, you won't know where your last paycheck went, your credit cards will be charged up to the maximum, and you'll have very little if anything in your savings account.

It's difficult to change yourself from a spender to a saver, or from a saver to a spender. It's your business which one you are, although I will give you a good piece of advice: When you are dating and/or choosing a significant other to marry, make sure you ask questions to acknowledge and understand each other's thinking and feelings about money. The last thing you would want is for the two of you to have regular and frequent conflicts about earning, spending, and saving money.

## Your Financial Planner Needs to Know

No one needs to know your personal business—except your financial planner.

The long-term financial goals of a saver and a spender can be very similar, but the strategies to achieve them are very different.

Example: Keepng it simple. You're a saver. I tell you to open a brokerage account having a mutual fund that will accept deposits of as little as $25 a week. You open the account. You put the $25 in each week. It's a good strategy for you because you're a saver.

If I make the same suggestion to a spender, he or she might get around to opening the account, but it's very unlikely that the weekly deposits of $25 will ever be made, or they will be made only after all of the other bills and expenses have been taken care of.

This is a bad strategy because the spender won't implement it.

Elsewhere in this book I talk about taking an equity line of credit on your home—having the account available in case you have a financial emergency. Would I recommend that strategy to a saver? Probably. Would I recommend it to a spender? Probably not. The available credit will be used on non-necessities, most likely, and our spender will then have mortgage and equity credit line payments to make each month.

I always spend time talking with each new client about goals and to determine if he or she is a spender or a saver. I want to be able to design the right plan for each client, and more importantly, I want some assurance that the client will follow the plan.

I said earlier that it's your business whether you're a spender or saver. Probably in your day-to-day life it doesn't matter which one; you've grown accustomed to spending or saving and you may find it difficult to change. However, you have to take full responsibility for yourself and your finances. You will be able to take on and carry out that responsibility better if you are a saver, or if you are willing to start a savings plan.

Throughout this book I will mention small, easy ways to start saving. Bring your lunch to work. Clip coupons. Have dinner parties at home rather than going out to expensive restaurants. But following these tips won't do much to help you build a solid savings account if you simply fritter your savings away on other things.

The key is to take the money you've saved each day or each week, and put it in a savings account—or other long term account I talked about earlier that accepts $25 or $50 deposits. A few dollars here and there, every day or two, quickly begin to add up. In fact, you may enjoy watching your account grow so much that you'll be inspired to deposit even more each week.

## SIMON SAYS...

In other words, whether you're a spender or saver, you can have a solid, achievable financial plan that fits your style of managing money. And even the spender can find simple, easy ways to start putting his or her money to work in some type of investment. Having discipline and vision to determine what's important long term is a process to work for and achieve.

◆

# SIMON SAYS: KNOW HOW TO USE THE RULE OF 72

◆

WANT TO FIGURE OUT how compound interest can double your money? It's easy. The Rule of 72 is a simple math formula that you can use two ways:

1. How long will it take to double your money at a given interest rate?

2. What interest rate do you have to get to double your money in a given number of years?

The rule is: Divide 72 by the "given" number you have—either annual interest rate or number of years—to approximate the unknown number.

Let's say that you plan to put $5,000 into a savings account at your local bank, which is paying 3% annual interest. How many years of earning interest at that annual rate will it take for your money to double—to grow into $10,000?

Answer: Divide 72 by the "given" number of 3% interest. The answer is 24 years.

Your response is, "Wow! Twenty-four years! That's too long! I want it to double by the time I retire in nine years!"

The question, then, is what annual rate of return will you have to earn for the next nine years in order to have your money double by the time you retire?

Answer: Divide 72 by the "given" number of nine years. The answer is 8% annual return. For your money to double in nine years, you need to get a return of 8% per year.

In both of these examples above, we've made the assumption that the interest rate will be locked in for that period of time—that it will never go up or down in the periods of nine years or twenty-four years we've used here.

To be realistic, there just aren't many investment choices available to you that will guarantee or lock in a specific interest rate on your money over a long period of time. It's a valuable exercise, though, because it makes us think in terms of long-term investments and long-term results. If you had been counting on your $10,000 inheritance from Aunt Millie to double in five years when you'll need the money for a fancy cruise you plan to take, you'll have to find a bank or credit union that will pay—and guarantee to keep paying for five years—an annual interest rate of almost 15%. That's not going to happen unless we have hyperinflation, which is something that no one wants. So now you know you have to go to Plan B—whatever that might be—to get the additional money you need for your cruise.

When I work with my clients to develop their financial plans, I keep reminding them to think long-term. We're planning for five, 10, 20 years from now. I use the "Rule of 72" to demonstrate that a sound financial strategy for long-term planning has to be much more diverse than putting all of the money into CDs.

## SIMON SAYS...

When my clients use the interest rates that CDs are earning these days—even longer-term CDs—in the "Rule of 72," they understand what I mean. As of this writing, five-year CDs are paying less than two percent interest. Using the Rule of 72, they can see that it will take thirty-six years for their investment to double. They understand that they will really need a well-researched, balanced portfolio of different types of investments with various levels of risk that will give them an income for the rest of their lives. They won't get that from investing in CDs.

◆

# SIMON SAYS:
# INCREASE YOUR
# FINANCIAL IQ

◆

SO YOU THINK YOU KNOW a lot about money, eh? You're not alone. Most folks figure that they know enough about money and finances to get them through life. In fact, they're probably right. With the basic information, you can do okay.

Of course, most of us want to do much better than just "okay." Certainly we want the comforts of a good place to live, enough food on the table, a car to drive, and clothing for ourselves and our children. Most of us dream of doing better than our parents or grandparents, and we hope that our children will do better than us. We want our children to have some of the luxuries of life, and we want to provide them with an advanced education—maybe MBA or Ph.D.

If you want to do better than just "okay," then you need to spend some time learning about personal finances. You need to understand the stock market. You need to take advantage of home ownership and the deductibility of mortgage interest from your tax returns. You need to purchase life insurance and to know at least a little about a lot of subjects.

The bottom line is that you'll never be able to make the best decisions—the right choices—about your personal finances if you don't know what all the choices are, how they work, and the right questions to ask so you can get the information you need.

You'll certainly learn a bit about a variety of financial topics in this book. When you work with a professional financial planner, you'll get even more information and answers, and you'll get an easy-to-understand explanation of how and why things work the way they do and how to roll them all together for your maximum financial benefit.

But if you're like the proverbial ostrich hiding your head in the sand and saying, "I don't make enough money to have to worry about how to spend it," or "I've done okay so far without any knowing a lot of sophisticated financial terms and topics," then it's possible you'll likely miss out on some great opportunities to become more financially savvy.

When you're done reading this book, I urge you to go to the library or bookstore to get a copy of *Rich Dad, Poor Dad* by Robert Kiyosaki. He reveals how he learned about money from the two major influences in his life—his father, who was highly educated yet who lived from paycheck to paycheck; and the father of his best friend, who was an eighth grade dropout and a multimillionaire. Kiyosaki makes us look at and think about money in an entirely different way than most of us would ever have considered, and he explores the belief that you need to earn a *high income* to become *rich*.

## SIMON SAYS...

You may or may not agree with his philosophy and recommendations for personal money management, but you'll have a totally new perspective on what money is all about and how to make it work for you. Second, turn to a coach, a certified financial planner™ practitioner to tailor a specific plan based upon your needs, circumstances, and risk tolerance. I do this everyday and truly love educating people. Financial Planning is like a puzzle of coordinating your insurance, investment, taxes, college, retirement and estate planning so that it is most effective for you. My clients have told me this is overwhelming and very difficult to do on their own. Simon says turn to a coach, get a second opinion, and please take responsibility for your money.

◆

# SIMON SAYS:
# USE FINANCIAL PLANNING
# TIPS AND TOOLS

◆

Would you wander through an unfamiliar forest without a path? Would you build a house without blueprints?

As Yogi Berra said, "If you don't know where you are going, you'll wind up somewhere else."

So if you want to have financial security, you must have a plan in place and choose the right tools to put your plan into action. It doesn't matter whether your bank balance is a number with no zeros or lots of zeros. It doesn't matter if you keep your cash in a piggy bank or in a vault at a big bank. It's important to keep track of your money and have a plan to preserve it and make it grow.

Don't assume that because you don't have millions that you can't use the strategies that are available to the wealthy. All of the laws, provisions, and financial planning tools that rich people use are available to everyone! It's true that some strategies—like setting up a trust— will cost money. Nevertheless, a trust can provide many benefits that can make a real difference for you, your family, and in the future. Trusts are not just for the rich. Trusts are not that complicated and can be very beneficial in your financial planning. In fact, I'll bet you currently have a trust. If you own an IRA account, that's a trust. Of course this type of trust has restrictions; if you take money out of this account before 59½ there is a 10% penalty, and you must take a required amount out at the age of 70½.

Here's another example. The IRS says in Section 101 of the Tax Code that life insurance proceeds may pass to your beneficiaries without them paying a single penny of income tax on those proceeds. In other words, life insurance provides immediate wealth to your heirs without any burdensome income taxes to be paid or loans to be repaid. How terrific is that?

Please note that Section 101 of the Tax Code does *not* say, "... only if you're rich." It's a regulation that's available to anyone and everyone who owns life insurance.

You need to know about these tools, these provisions, and these strategies. When you know they're out there—available to you—you can ask your professional financial planner which ones apply to you, the advantages and disadvantages of each, and how to make these tools work for you.

## SIMON SAYS...

Don't think for a moment that, if you're not rich, then you don't need or can't use the same strategies and tools that wealthy people use. You do need them and you can benefit from them. You'll reap the same advantages as the wealthy folks!

P.S. Even Wealthy people don't think they're wealthy.

◆

# SIMON SAYS:
# WORK WITH A PRO

◆

YOU MAY BE A TALENTED auto mechanic. A courteous customer service representative. The best dentist east of the Mississippi River, or an accomplished attorney or doctor.

Does being a good engineer also mean that you know and understand complex financial matters? Would your expertise as an airline pilot guarantee that you can avoid the potential pitfalls and sort out tax implications of the various types of investment vehicles?

Although some people do successfully manage, invest, and grow their money, most people have only a basic understanding of the complexities of sophisticated financial and retirement planning. And some of those who try to manage and invest on their own end up making some very expensive mistakes.

As one of my colleagues is fond of saying, "Even Tiger Woods has a coach."

## Finding and Selecting a
## Professional Financial Planner

You need to be working with a professional financial planner, and you don't need to be wealthy to have one. If you don't have money, they will show you how to accumulate it. If you do have money, they will help you protect it and make it grow.

But how can you find one?

One idea is to turn to the Internet. You'll find large and small websites, major firms and sole practitioners, independent advisors and those exclusively affiliated with one bank or investment firm. How can you possibly choose the right one for you by looking at a bunch of websites?

A much better method is to talk to your friends, family members, golfing buddies, as well as the other professional advisors who coach you—your lawyer and your accountant or your mortgage planner. Ask whom they use or recommend. Ask what they like and don't like about the planner they work with. Ask if their planner is knowledgeable, experienced, and trustworthy.

Before you make your decision, be sure to meet with two or three advisors. It's essential that you interview each advisor you're considering. You'll be trusting him or her to help you make some important decisions. You'll want to know:

- **Education and professional designations**. A planner who is committed to his or her clients wants to keep learning. He or she completes advanced study in specialized subjects having to do with financial planning. The courses are usually offered by professional organizations in the financial planning field. Once the planner successfully completes the study and has passed an exam, he or she can use the professional designations to show advanced expertise. Look for designations such as certified financial planner™ practitioner (CFP), chartered life underwriter (CLU), chartered financial consultant (CHFC), certified fund specialist (CFS), and registered financial consultant (RFC), which appear after the planner's name on his or her letterhead, business cards, and other professional documents.

- **Experience.** The length of time a planner has been in practice can only enhance your success in working with this person. This advisor will bring his or her experience from working with many people that are in a similar situation to yours, and they have an understanding of the next phase you'll be experiencing. You should expect to work with your financial planner—to help fund your children's college education; to grow your nest egg for retirement; have sufficient life, health and long-term care insurance for financial security, elder law planning for your parents and yourself, and to help set up an estate plan to transfer assets to your benefactors.

So it may be difficult to evaluate how "successful" a planner is if they've only been in business for a few years. You will want to be reassured that he or she can help you with all phases of your financial planning because they have helped hundreds of other clients. Experience counts for a lot in this profession.

◆ **Personal and professional "style" and philosophy.** Will you be comfortable working with a "cowboy" who recommends that you make high-risk investments? Do you want your planner to be very formal and conservative? Will you want your planner to take the time to educate you on the key elements to have a diversified plan? You need to work with someone you can trust and respect, with the same values and outlook as yours. Take the time to find the planner with whom you feel most comfortable.

◆ **Research and support.** Even a dedicated financial planner can't know everything about every type of investment, every return of every fund, every provision and exclusion of every long-term care insurance policy on the market today. You'll want a planner who has experts and resources to call upon. If your planner is with a large firm, those resources may be on the premises. If your planner is a sole practitioner, he or she should be affiliated in some manner with a broker/dealer, insurance company, or investment firm, and have access to that firm's research and support.

◆ **Method of payment.** In the old days, most financial planners were compensated by earning a commission on every sale. The client didn't pay any money out-of-pocket. That's changing now. Today you'll find a growing number of financial planners who have switched to fee-based planning. The advantage is that you can be sure that your planner's recommendations are those that are best for you—rather than those that pay him or her the biggest commission. Fee-based planners are less likely to be "sales people" and more like attorneys and accountants who are paid for their time, education and expertise.

As the planner's potential client, you need to know how he or she will be compensated for working with you and that you're comfortable with it—before you enter into a professional relationship.

You may be interested to know, from my perspective as a Certified Financial Planner™ practitioner, while you're in my office interviewing me, I'm interviewing you. I want to know how serious you are about developing a financial plan. Are you committed to carrying out a plan, even if there are some ups and downs in the short-term markets? Will you be open to learning what I'm suggesting? I want you to be able to understand, trust, and use this information. I tell people up front that I may not always agree with what they want. It's my job to provide you with objective information and advice; if I'm not comfortable with your requests I need to tell you that. I'll always be honest and then say, "It's your money and of course you'll do with it what you decide."

## SIMON SAYS...

You can't be good at everything. You don't need to be wealthy or nearing retirement to work with a qualified, experienced, professional planner. In fact, you may benefit even more from coaching if you're not wealthy and if you have a long time to go before retirement.

◆

# SIMON SAYS:
# PLANNING IS A PROCESS

◆

YOU'RE PROBABLY FAMILIAR with the standard estate planning documents including the will, trust, power of attorney, and living wills. You've taken great care to ensure these instruments are properly drawn and will stand the test of time.

For your legacy to flourish, you need to remember that these documents and assets will be interpreted and administered by human beings, and that your beneficiaries are people who will be looking at their inheritance through their own personal prism. In addition, life changes, and no part of your plan is static. Those documents that you carefully constructed five years ago may be woefully out of date. The people whom you have entrusted to carry out your legacy may be sick, passed away or your relationship may have changed and your children or beneficiaries may now be responsible to carry out your wishes. Planning is a process that even when completed needs regular review.

Here are six tips that Simon says will help you plan effectively.

1. **Plan for the three key people**. Concern for all the technical questions involving laws, taxes, and paperwork is fine, but does not mean your support network is in place. The three key roles are **financial adviser, accountant**, and **attorney**. Ensure that your estate plan has these three roles filled by people you specifically designate. Select these advisers carefully and include them in your planning. This will ensure that the team is ready well in advance of your death or disability. I as a certified financial planner™ practitioner act as a quarterback to confirm all the i's are dotted and t's are crossed. I also want to confirm the titling/ownership of the assets are coordinated with the language of your legal documents.

2. **Consider distribution**. Every legacy includes three parts: To whom, how much, and when. There is an art to putting together a distribution plan that works for both your estate and your heirs. Distribution timing, incentives and disincentives, and asset protection for unexpected disasters carry implications that extend beyond the obvious desires of avoiding taxes and probate. For example, should a college student inherit everything in one lump sum, or would staggered payments be more prudent? And what happens five years from now when the college student is now a college grad? How about your spouse, should he or she survive you? Should the family home be saved or put on the market? The more of these issues that can be delineated in advance, the better.

3. **Title and designate beneficiaries wisely.** This is a common mistake made in estate planning that can lead to unintended probates simply because assets are inadvertently left out of plans, or beneficiary lists are not kept current. No one can predict when an estate plan will go into effect, so it should always be up to date and accurate.

4. **Distribute based on percentages versus real dollars.** Thoughtful distribution may entail more than an exercise in mathematical percentages. Using actual numbers allows you to consider how much inheritance is enough and what is to be done with the remainder. On the other hand, if your estate fluctuates in value and you want to ensure that all of your heirs receive a proportional share, then basing your bequest on percentages makes sense. Ask yourself if funds need to be delineated for specific uses, such as an education trust, and if there need to be incentives for assets left in trust for following generations.

5. **Insure appropriately.** Too many estate plans are underinsured. While no one likes to pay for insurance, in estate planning the

risk of underinsuring needs to be recognized. More importantly, the life insurance needs to be owned properly. Life insurance is no longer a buy and hold asset; we are living longer and the mortality costs have been reduced. You must review these policies to determine your options for saving money or receiving increased protection as long as you're in good health. As I discuss in another chapter, insurance is an extremely helpful tool in estate planning, and needs to be used effectively.

6. **Make sure the right person does each job.** Trustees, executors, and those with power of attorney assume responsibilities that are critical to your legacy. Yet not everyone is equally skilled, or able, to handle these tasks. Social friends, adult children, or distant relatives may not be able to act, or be knowledgeable as an institutional trustee. You need to fairly balance the duties of the job with the person's actual skills and ability to handle problems, and there is no harm in reaching out to a professional.

7. **Update it.** Estate planning is an ongoing process, not a one-time event. Your plan is never set in stone. As people move forward in their careers, kids get older, assets change in value, your investing strategy shifts, houses are sold, and life changes occur, all plans become out of date. Simon says that at least once every few years you should review and update your estate plan documents and designations to reflect your current family's needs.

## SIMON SAYS...

Your legacy is a living entity. Don't put your legal documents in a drawer or stop the conversation—make sure you keep it current with changes in your life and the lives of your beneficiaries.

◆

# SIMON SAYS: REVIEW YOUR LIFE INSURANCE NEEDS

◆

WE ALL EXPECT TO LIVE TO A RIPE OLD AGE, and to keep working and providing our spouse and children with the necessities and perhaps a few luxuries in life. A reality check, however, shows us that the unexpected can happen at any time. Who would provide for your family and loved ones if you weren't around tomorrow?

A term life insurance policy can be an important part of your legacy. Obviously having life insurance won't help *you* after you die, because you have to die to collect it. But it gives you an incredible sense of security knowing that you have implemented a plan to protect your loved ones.

Term life insurance provides coverage for a specific length of time. And it's a bargain; only about one percent of all term life insurance policies are executed. That means that lots of people buy it and pay premiums, but only about one in a hundred die so that the insurance companies have to pay death benefits. Term life is especially inexpensive if you buy it when you're young and healthy—in your twenties or early thirties—because the risk or chance of you dying then is pretty small. As you get older and perhaps have health issues, the cost rises considerably because there's a higher risk of dying.

You can purchase term insurance for a set term—5, 10, 15, 20, or 30 years.

You have the option of "locking in" the premium for a set term period. You will have created a fixed expense in your monthly annual budget. You'll always know how much your premium payments will be, and for budgeting purposes, that's a big plus!

That also means that, as you get pay raises, bonuses, overtime pay, or other additional income, you don't have to hang onto it until you find out what your next life insurance premium will be, because you already know. Therefore, you can take that additional income and earmark it for tax-deductible retirement savings—that is, to increase or even max out your 401(k) contributions or any other contributory retirement plan available to you.

If you already have a term life insurance policy, you should ask yourself if your assets have lost value in the recent bear market.

Perhaps you have been planning to leave your assets to your children, grandchildren, or even a favorite charity. But because of the recent decline of the stock market, the assets you were counting on may have significantly diminished. Life insurance can help to replace or offset that loss, and many boomer singles and couples are buying it now for just that purpose.

## How Much Life Insurance Do You Have Now?

Most working people only have life insurance coverage through their employer, and they think that's enough. It's *not*!

In fact, when you're adding up the life insurance you already have in place, it's a good idea *not* to include any life insurance that your employer provides for you. Think of that as a "bonus," because it's probably not nearly enough as you really need, and because, if you leave the company, the life insurance they've provided for you will end. When and if your employment ends you may have the option of converting it from a company-owned policy to your own; ask the human resources manager at work about this. But it's going to be expensive, *very* expensive.

Besides, you can't count on being with the same employer for 20 years anymore; those days are gone. You need to take responsibility for protecting yourself and your family on your own. Simon says purchase your own life insurance.

A better idea is to get your own policy separately from what your employer provides—for mobility and security.

# How Much Life Insurance Do You Need?

When determining how much life insurance you need, the first step is to think about the different purposes that life insurance may have and how those relate to you, your family, and your goals. Some of the purposes are:

◆ Pay for funeral and related expenses.

◆ Pay off mortgage, credit cards and other debts

◆ Fund a college education.

◆ Long-term financial security, for your family (Income Replacement)

◆ Financial security for your family and other dependents. I've seen many clients caring for parents, and they too are dependent on your financial assistance. If you weren't here and there was no way to replace your income after your death, they would be left in the lurch.

◆ Financial gift to a favorite charity or organization.

◆ Financial investment and /or supplemental retirement income so your policy offers investment options while you're still alive. You can borrow against the cash value in the future.

◆ Financial strategy for business owners to fund buy/sell agreements.

◆ Liquidity to pay Estate Taxes or Income Tax on an IRA

There are two easy ways to help you estimate the amount of life insurance you need today. There is a rule of thumb that says to multiply your current annual income amount (the gross amount—before taxes) times ten to give you an amount. If you earn $50,000 per year, you should own about $500,000 of life insurance.

When I was growing up, $500,000 was a *lot* of money. Today it's not. So you may need to readjust your thinking and be realistic about the costs to live and take care of your family today and into the future. In my opinion, every breadwinner with a child or children should have at least one million dollars of life insurance. An old friend who is a trusted CPA named Ed Mendlowitz called it the "Mendlowitz Special," and so I call it the "Simon Says Special"—one million dollars of life insurance on you and make sure you have coverage on your spouse.

One million dollars sounds like a lot—maybe more than they might need. But consider the question of "want." How financially well off do you want to leave your loved ones? If you're like me, you want to make it a little easier for the next generation, as your parents have done for you. You can do that easily and affordably with term life insurance. Also, you don't want your loved ones struggling if some large, unforeseeable expenses come up in the future. Take care of this need today and be done with it! Please.

The other way to estimate how much you need is to use the following process, which should give you a much more accurate estimate of the amount of life insurance you personally should own.

1   List all of your financial liabilities. Liabilities include every debt and financial obligation that you have and that you and your spouse have jointly, such as your home mortgage(s). Include the balances you owe on all credit cards, the amount you owe on your car loan(s), educational loans, and home improvement. Think carefully to be sure you list everything, even if the amount owed is relatively small.

Add up those numbers to get the total amount of your debt that your surviving spouse or family members would need to pay off.

2. Calculate how much of your annual income your family would need to replace. For example, you pay the phone & utilities, auto insurance, property taxes, birthday gifts, and you provide money for clothes, food, furniture, and home repairs. You may need money for college for your children and for your own retirement; you need to add those numbers in as well. These recurring expenses is what your family will need per year to replace your income, and that amount will grow each year with inflation. It doesn't include paying off the debts that you listed in Step 1. For example, 1mm of life insurance at 4% direct interest would produce 40k of income a year.

3. If you have children and plan for them to attend college, add to your liability total (1 and 2 together) an amount equal to four years of college times the number of children. If your children will be attending college in the next five or less years, you can use $20,000 to $50,000 as an annual estimate; use higher numbers if your children are five to ten years away from attending college. Also read the tip about college planning, found in the section "Making your Money Grow".

4. Add up the total of your assets, including money in your individual and joint savings plan and investment accounts, money in your company's 401(k), 403(b), and/or profit-sharing that has vested, that belongs to you today. Include any stocks, bonds, and mutual funds at their current value. Do you own an antique car, jewelry, antiques, or valuable art work? A stamp or coin collection? Decide if you would want them to be liquidated or if you want them to stay in your family.

5. Subtract your assets from your liabilities. The resulting number is called your *net worth*. If you have more liabilities than assets, then your net worth may well be a negative number—and that's all the more reason to buy more life insurance, so that you won't burden your surviving spouse and family with a mountain of debt.

Another word to the wise: your spouse needs life insurance, too. He or she may or may not be working outside the home, but even if they're home with the children, they're working just as hard as you are—caring for the children, shopping, cooking meals, doing laundry to housekeeping, and everything else around the home. If something were to happen to your partner, you'd probably need to hire one or more people to do all of those things for you and your family.

While you're taking care of your own need for life insurance, be sure to do the same for your spouse. Are you part of the sandwich generation, which means you may be taking care of your parents, children, aunts, uncles and maybe even siblings? When doing your life insurance calculation, remember to determine who is relying on you financially.

## Refinance Your Life Insurance

With the very low interest rates we've been seeing for the past few years, almost everyone has refinanced their mortgages to get a lower rate of interest and lower monthly payments.

What about life insurance? You can do the same thing. Rates have come down dramatically in the past few years because people are living longer. Talk to your financial planner about the simple steps you can take to save yourself some money by lowering your premium payments.

While you're at it, ask your financial planner to be sure that your life insurance is properly owned—preferably in an irrevocable life insurance trust. (See chapter on trusts) If it's not properly owned, now is the time to review it. By putting it into a trust, the proceeds of the policy are income tax free, estate tax free, and protected from creditors and predators. Always verify and update your beneficiaries.

## SIMON SAYS...

The way to refinance your life insurance is to forfeit your old policy with the high premiums and buy a new policy with the same or even more coverage. You'll go through the same process of applying, (blood work & having a health exam), and so on that you did for your first policy. But you'll save money and you'll have more protection for your family. Never give up your old policy before obtaining your new one.

◆

# SIMON SAYS:
# USE LIFE INSURANCE AS A
# FINANCIAL PLANNING TOOL

◆

I'VE TALKED ABOUT THE ESSENTIAL NEED to own life insurance so that you can protect your family and provide them with financial security if something were to happen to you. Your life insurance would replace the income that you had been earning and would pay off your mortgage(s) and your debts. It would also fund college expenses for your children, assuring them of a higher education even if you're not around to pay for it.

But life insurance can also be a powerful financial planning tool to help you accomplish some other important objectives. Here are just a few:

◆ Immediately create an estate for your children, grandchildren, other dependents, or a favorite charity.

◆ Provide Liquidity and help pay estate taxes on a discounted basis.

◆ Create an additional source of income at retirement by accessing the cash value of your life insurance. If done the right way, it's tax free.

◆ For business owners, life insurance can be an excellent funding vehicle for deferred compensation planning. It can be especially useful when used for retaining key employees. The employee gets a retirement benefit and the business eventually is repaid its investment via proceeds from the death benefits. Big corporations have been using this strategy for years and taking advantage of the actuarial likelihood that they will be reimbursed for their costs.

Also for business owners, life insurance is the most effective vehicle for funding the owners' obligations under a buy/sell agreement with tax-free dollars.

♦ Provide financial protection if you become ill or disabled. For example, if you should be diagnosed with a serious disease, the costs associated with this illness may include treatment, loss of income, withdrawals from your 401k Plan, travel, and accommodation costs for treatment. These costs can even drive you into bankruptcy if you do not have resources in place to handle them.

I'm a strong advocate of life insurance for a lot of reasons, and when I work with my clients to develop a long-term financial and retirement plan, some type of life insurance is always a key element.

## SIMON SAYS...

If you've always thought of life insurance only for death benefits, it's time to re-think your position. Read and Learn. Talk to your financial advisor or contact me directly—my contact information is at the end of this book. The more you know, the more you can take advantage of some of these features of permanent life insurance.

♦

# SIMON SAYS: LEARN ABOUT LONG-TERM CARE INSURANCE

◆

BECAUSE OF HEALTHY LIVING, better nutrition, excellent health care, medications, state-of-the-art equipment and tools for diagnosis and treatment, we Americans are living longer than any generation in the history of our country.

That's the good news.

The bad news is that because we're living longer, we're increasingly suffering from long-term health problems or debilitating conditions such as arthritis or Alzheimer's disease. As a result, it's estimated that 50% of people age 85 and older will need some type of assistance either in their home or in a facility such as a nursing home.

Ask anyone you know and they'll probably say that they want to continue to live in their home for as long as they possibly can, even if illness or infirmity should afflict them; and I feel the same way.

We all need to face reality. Too many folks assume that either they won't need long-term care or that they can receive the care they'll need at home from their spouse, children or other family members. But then you have to ask yourself, "Do I want to be a burden to my spouse? Do I want my children or grandchildren bathing me?" Most people say "no" to those questions.

Furthermore, you have to consider whether or not your spouse will be physically able to care for you at home when the time comes. Will he or she be healthy, strong, and capable of taking on the responsibilities of caring for you? Will his or her health seriously deteriorate from the stress of trying to care for you? And what happens then—to you and to your spouse?

Long-term care insurance allows us the choice to remain at home because it will pay for professional care in your own home as well as in a skilled nursing facility, assisted living residence, or a nursing home. It will pay for professional care so that you don't force your spouse or adult child to try to give you the care you need. You'll have the freedom to choose the kind of care you get and where you get it.

Above and beyond the choices of how and where we get our care, this insurance also helps us preserve our assets—our savings, our investments, and other assets we want to pass along to our loved ones. I recommend that you talk to your financial advisor about it sooner rather than later.

## What Are the Options?

In my opinion, too many people try to "self insure" for long-term care expenses. In other words, they don't buy the insurance, but figure that (a) they won't need any long-term care (hopefully! good luck!), or (b) they'll stay at home and have a loved one care for them (and have your spouse's health deteriorate or be a burden to your children), or (c) Medicaid will pay all of those bills for them. But Medicaid rules may mean that you need to be absolutely broke and living now in conditions you'd rather not be in. Medicaid may also place restrictions on the level and type of care you receive and/or the quality of the nursing home or assisted living facility.

As you age, will your children be able to care for you in your home?

Will you have sufficient assets on hand to take care of those expenses two, ten or twenty years from now?

Most people don't have nearly enough in accessible or liquid assets to cover those costs, and the financial burdens that encumber families because of this growing health care need can totally exhaust their assets.

You could certainly start saving now—putting aside money into an Individual Retirement Account (IRA) for example. But when you need it to pay for long-term care (or anything else), it's taxed as ordinary income—as much as 40%, for example—leaving little more than half of your IRA savings to pay for long-term care. Check with your accountant regarding deductibility of medical expenses. (Currently, if Medical Expenses are above 7.5% of your AGI, you can take a deduction).

A much more efficient financial planning tool is an insurance policy that will create a pool of money to be available when you need it for long-term care, so that you can have the same dignity, independence, and self-respect that you had when you were able to function and take care of yourself. It has been said we come into the world as a baby and leave as a baby—and if that's true, we'll need the same assistance and care from a loved one as we once received when we were born.

# What Exactly Is Long-Term Care Insurance?

A long-term care insurance policy will provide you with cash to help with the costs of long-term care. When you purchase a policy, you can choose among many options. One is the waiting period before the policy kicks in—say, 90 days of your first receiving care. That's similar to a deductible with your auto or homeowner insurance; you pay 100% of the expenses until the plan kicks in. The longer the waiting period you choose, the lower your premium will be because you'll be paying for a larger portion of your own care than you would if you chose 60 days, for example.

To determine if you're eligible for benefits under your plan, your physician will determine that you are not able to handle two of the six "Activities of Daily Living," as they're called. The six ADLs are:

1. Eating
2. Bathing
3. Dressing
4. Toileting
5. Transferring
6. Maintaining continence

# How Much Does
# Long-Term Care Insurance Cost?

The quick and best answer to this question is, "It costs less than long-term care!"

Let's look at the costs for long-term care today. Depending on where you live in the United States, cost for around-the-clock care could be as high as $300 per day—that's over $100,000 per year. And those are today's costs. Always recommend to add an inflation feature of 3-5% so the Daily Benefit increases annually.

The younger you are when you purchase LTC insurance, the cheaper it is. Remember, There are several factors in determining the cost of long-term care insurance, including:

- Your age at the time you purchase it.

- The dollar amount of benefits you want per day or month.

- How long you want coverage to protect you at the time you qualify (meeting the 2 of 6 ADL's, activities for daily living), to run for three years, five years or unlimited coverage?

As with most other types of insurance, if you don't use it, you'll lose it. However, for an additional fee, you can purchase a non-forfeiture benefit rider that will refund all the premiums you've paid if you don't use the coverage. This rider is very expensive, and I recommend to my clients that, instead of purchasing it, they take the same amount of dollars and invest them in a growth-oriented mutual fund. Over time, the investment will grow and offset what you've paid in premiums, whether or not you use your LTC insurance benefits.

How much does long-term care insurance cost? You'll be surprised, I think, to find that it costs considerably less than what most folks would guess. For example, here are some numbers for long-term care insurance from a well-established, reputable insurance company. These numbers are based on the following assumptions. They are provided only as a general reference and do not represent an offer. Figures may change based on an individuals age & insurability.

| | |
|---|---|
| Maximum Daily Benefit: | $200 per day |
| Home Care Payment Option: | Monthly benefit |
| Home Care % of Max. Daily Benefit: | 100% |
| Inflation Protection | 3% Compound |
| Benefit Period: | 5 years |
| Lifetime Maximum Benefit Amount: | $360,000 |
| Elimination (waiting) Period: | 90 day |
| | |
| Resident of: | New Jersey |
| Male, age 45: | $2,100 |
| | Total Annual Premium |
| Male, age 55: | $2,500 |
| | Total Annual Premium |
| Male, age 70: | $6,900 |
| | Total Annual Premium |

As you can see, waiting is expensive!

# How Should You Pay for LTC Insurance?

Most people think that they should pay the premiums for long-term care insurance from their monthly disposable income. Simon says look at paying for the insurance from your assets, your net worth.

Remember, this isn't disability insurance to protect your income. The reason to own the long term care insurance is to protect your assets and your net worth.

# Plan Ahead

## SIMON SAYS...

Communicate with your family now. Start the process while you're still years away from needing any type of long-term care. Don't let money be a real issue when it comes to the planning required. Too many people wait until it's too late, and when that conversation finally takes place, everyone feels they are working under pressure.

The best approach is to start when you and your children are relatively young and healthy. It eases the stress and tension, and opens up the "money barrier" conversation more comfortably. Seek professional advice in your state regarding current Medicaid regulations and elder care law. When you provide for proper elder law planning and get everything settled, then everyone is happy.

◆

# SIMON SAYS:
# PLAN TO PASS ON
# FINANCIAL RESPONSIBILITY

◆

NO ONE WANTS TO GET OLD or face their own mortality. But when you're building your financial legacy, you're doing so with the implicit recognition that Benjamin Franklin was quite right when he said that nothing was certain in life except death and taxes. The inevitable fact is that as you grow older, important tasks such as overseeing your finances may become more difficult to manage alone. Certain medical issues may make a task as familiar as writing checks or balancing your accounts too difficult. And a chronic condition such as Alzheimer's disease can erode sound decision-making, potentially jeopardizing your hard-earned savings.

Regardless of the circumstances, there's a strong possibility that you'll eventually need to take a simple but personally difficult action: handing control of your finances to someone you trust. This is not something that you want to do at the eleventh hour. If you're thoroughly prepared for that moment, you're more likely to experience a smooth transition.

## When to Hand Over Control

Identifying the time when it's necessary to transfer control of finances—either yours or a loved one's—isn't always easy. We like to see ourselves not only as living to a ripe old age and beyond (death is something that happens to other people), but as rugged individualists who are self sufficient and don't need "babysitting." But for the clear-headed individual, there are indications of when a partial handover of responsibilities may be necessary. These can include symptoms that are obvious but tempting to deny such as physical, cognitive, or psychological impairments. You might have shaky hands that make it difficult to fill out documents, or memory loss that makes it difficult to manage a budget.

Do you have to give up everything all at once? No. Yielding responsibility may at first take the form of asking a trusted individual such as a son or daughter to come over occasionally to help with basic tasks, and then eventually involve handing full control of finances to a family member or legal guardian.

A smooth transition is key. Without the proper structure in place, older people having trouble managing their finances can experience some unfortunate and potentially tragic consequences. For instance, forgetting to pay bills may lead to disconnected utilities. And another serious concern is vulnerability to fraud.

## Power of Attorney and Irrevocable Trust

You can help avoid risk by preparing a legal structure ahead of time that allows for a trusted individual to make decisions that are in your financial best interests. The most common—and most important—document in this process is a durable power of attorney. It designates somebody you trust—the principal—to handle your routine financial affairs. In most cases, a durable power of attorney allows you to designate specific financial transactions for which your agent is responsible. These may include such things as managing investments, writing checks, and handling tax returns.

While a power of attorney serves an important role in transferring control, individuals with complicated financial situations or significant wealth often require additional legal mechanisms. A common way for wealthy individuals to create a mechanism for managing assets is through an irrevocable trust. A qualified person is designated as trustee, and that person has power to manage assets such as real estate, businesses, or stocks that have been placed in the trust.

# Plan Ahead

Regardless of how you eventually transfer control of your finances, you should prepare for the transfer long before it happens. While it's never too late to start, it's wise to have discussions early on with your family about what needs to be done if and when you become unable to make financial decisions on your own. You even can start as soon as you get married, or when you have children. The steps needed to facilitate a smooth transition of financial control should take place years or decades before the signs of debilitation become apparent.

## SIMON SAYS...

Talk to your financial planner about designating a person to handle your finances if and when you become unable to do so. Discuss the steps necessary to draft a power of attorney and how to place some of your assets in an irrevocable trust. By doing so, you'll be protecting your financial legacy for the next generation.

◆

# TRUSTS

◆

# NOTES

# SIMON SAYS:
# LEARN ABOUT TRUSTS

◆

WHEN YOU PASS AWAY, you want to leave a financial legacy for your spouse, children or grandchildren. It's a very good idea, but you have to manage the process properly.

In an earlier chapter, I said that when planning your bequest you need to answer three big questions: To whom, how much, and when. Right now I'll talk about "when." And the best way to think about the "when" is to consider the form in which you transfer your assets.

The form of your bequest can vary greatly. At one extreme, you could bequeath to your heirs a big pot of cash. Your heirs could take the big pot of cash and buy a Rolls-Royce. And there you go—fifty years of your hard work instantly converted into a sweet ride for your kid and his crew. In this case, the answer to the question of "when" would be *"now!"*

As you can imagine, there are big problems with this approach. The two most serious concerns are: 1. You may not want Junior to have his inheritance in one fell swoop; and 2. Handing over a big pot of cash may have significant tax implications.

This is why many loving parents and grandparents set up trusts. Put simply, a trust agreement is a document that controls the flow of assets that your heirs will either benefit from or eventually own outright. Think of a trust as a special place into which assets from your estate are placed, and thereby acquire immunity from estate taxes, become resistance to probate, be given a new definition of ownership, and so on.

To understand trusts, you need to understand one basic concept: there is a difference between being a *beneficiary* of something and *owning* it. A trust allows one person to benefit from the assets in the trust while another person retains legal ownership. It's like a tenant who leases an apartment from a landlord: both parties have legally defined and binding rights. And, like a tenant–landlord lease, most trusts have a defined time limitation. They don't last forever.

To set up a trust, you need six basic elements:

1.  **Person funding the trust.** This would be you. Commonly known as the trustor; also grantor, donor, or settlor.

2.  **Type of trust.** Trusts come in many different varieties, which I'll cover in subsequent chapters.

3.  **Assets.** Could be cash, stocks, securities, real estate, business interests, intellectual material, fine art—just about anything of value.

4.  **Beneficiary.** The individual(s) who benefit from the trust in some way. After a predetermined time period, they may or may not take ownership of the assets.

5.  **Trustee.** The person who has legal authority over the trust is known as the trustee. The trustee could be an individual or the trust department of your bank.

6.  **Rules.** Many of the rules that must be followed are inherently part of the type of trust chosen. Others depend on what is specified in the trust agreement, and still others rest in state and federal law.

## Why Set Up a Trust?

Here are some common benefits and objectives of using trusts:

♦   **Protect your estate** (and your beneficiary's or beneficiaries' estate). See the Rolls-Royce example, above. A trust can direct assets to a particular beneficiary over a period of time. It can also protect the principle from falling into the ownership of someone else (such as your heir's spouse).

◆ **Reduce taxes.** There may be tax advantages to holding assets in a trust rather than gifting them outright to your heirs.

◆ **Avoid probate.** By keeping certain property out of your probate estate, you may be able to avoid many of the costs and complications related to probate.

◆ **Provide funds for educational purposes.** Trusts can make funds available to your children or anyone whom you designate for educational purposes including college tuition and living expenses.

◆ **Benefit charities and non-profit institutions.** A charitable trust can annually provide money to a charity or organization. This can begin while you're still alive and then continue after your death.

## SIMON SAYS...

A trust need not be expensive or complicated to be effective. Whether it's large or small, a trust is a way to manage the controlled disbursement of your assets over time, and ensure that your legacy has the maximum impact.

◆

# SIMON SAYS:
# KNOW THE TYPES
# OF TRUSTS

◆

B ECAUSE TRUSTS ARE BY DEFINITION an asset held by
one person or entity for the benefit of another, they come in all
shapes and sizes, and serve many purposes. In this chapter I'll intro-
duce you to some of the most common forms of trusts that are used
to convey wealth from one generation to another. These are just the
basic structures; your financial advisor and trust attorney can create a
trust expressly for your needs.

Before I get to specific trusts, I should mention that you may hear
the term "express trust." An express trust is simply one where the
trustor or settlor (you) deliberately chooses to create a trust. You're
not forced to do it by a court or other outside entity. You create an
express trust by signing a trust document (this can be either be your
will or a trust deed). Almost all trusts are express trusts; other broad
categories of trusts include resulting trusts, implied trusts, and con-
structive trusts, which are generally not relevant to the purpose of
leaving your legacy.

Here are some common forms of express trusts. In subsequent
chapters I'll discuss them in greater detail.

◆ **Annuity trust.** This type of trust pays to your heirs a fixed amount
every year. As determined when the trust is established, the annual
amount must be at least five percent of the initial fair market value
of the trust's assets. Contrast this to the **unitrust,** below.

◆ **Bypass trust.** In the United States, a bypass trust is an irrevocable trust that is designed to pay trust income and/or principal
to your spouse for the duration of your spouse's life. The transfer

of assets to the bypass trust for the benefit of your spouse is tax-free, and upon your death, the assets in the bypass trust are not included in your estate.

- **Directed trust.** Normally, one trustee is sufficient to oversee a trust. However, in our increasingly complex world of financial management, an increasing number of high net worth individuals are creating trusts governed by multiple participants or agents, each of whom has a specialty. Together these participants have carefully defined authority to direct the activities of the trustee.

- **Dynasty trust, or generation-skipping trust**. In a dynasty trust, eventual ownership of the assets is passed down to your grandchildren, skipping your children. Your children never take title to the assets. There may be some estate tax advantages to a generation-skipping trust. Your children need not be cut out completely; the income from the trust can be disbursed to your children, while leaving the assets intact to be given to your grandchildren on a certain date or under other designated conditions.

- **Fixed trust.** In a fixed trust, you designate what your heirs are to receive. The trustee has little or no power to make changes. Some common examples of fixed trusts are:
  - A remainder trust, which grants a specific sum to the heir(s) upon your death.
  - A trust for a minor, in which the heir receives the assets when he or she reaches a certain age. A Section 2503(c) Minor's Trust is a trust established to hold assets in trust for a child until the child reaches age 21. The trust is named after the section of the Internal Revenue Code upon which it is based.
  - A life interest, in which the heir receives a sum at regular intervals, such as monthly or quarterly.

- **Hybrid trust.** This type involves paying fixed amounts to your heirs, with the assumption that there may be a sum left over. Once the fixed amounts have been paid out, the trustee may then determine how any remaining assets are to be paid to your heirs.

- **Incentive trust.** If you want to establish conditions that must be met by your heir or heirs, an incentive trust uses asset distributions as an incentive to either encourage or discourage certain behaviors. You may wish, for example, that your child earn a college degree before receiving benefits from the trust. In contrast, a **discretionary trust** may leave such decisions up to the trustee.

- **Intentionally defective grantor trust (IDGT).** It's not really defective; it just means that you continue to pay income taxes on the assets in the trust, because the IRS does not recognize that assets have been transferred away from your control. However, for estate tax purposes the value of your estate is reduced by the amount of the asset transfer.

- ***Inter vivos* trust, or living trust.** This simply means that the trust has been established while you're still alive, rather than upon your death.

- **Irrevocable trust.** This means that the terms of the trust cannot be revised or amended until the terms or purposes of the trust have been fulfilled. An irrevocable trust may not be altered by the trustee or the beneficiaries of the trust. In rare cases, a court may change the terms of the trust because unanticipated changes have made the trust difficult to administer or uneconomical.

- **Life insurance trust.** A life insurance trust is an irrevocable trust in which the primary asset is your life insurance policy. Upon your death, the trustee invests the proceeds from the insurance policy and administers the resulting assets in the trust for one or more beneficiaries.

♦ **Offshore trust.** A commonly used term used describing a trust located in a tax haven.

♦ **Private and public trusts.** In a private trust, you name one or more of your heirs as beneficiaries. In a public trust (also called a **charitable trust**), you name a charitable organization as the beneficiary. For example, a charitable trust may be set up to benefit a museum, church, or hospital. The charity may receive only the income from the trust, or a percentage of its value, or, at some date, the assets themselves.

♦ **Protective trust.** A form of irrevocable living trust used when you need to shield assets from a creditor or other third party. Assets placed into the protective trust no longer belong to you.

♦ **Revocable living trust.** A form of living trust that may be altered, amended, or revoked by you at any time, provided you are not mentally incapacitated. In the United States, to reduce administrative costs associated with probate and to provide efficient administration of a person's estate, revocable trusts are becoming increasingly common as a substitute for wills. Revocable living trusts that spell out how you want your assets managed while you're alive and distributed after your death are quickly becoming the preferred form of estate plan for many families.

♦ **Simple trust.** There are two different meanings. In a simple trust the trustee has no responsibilities beyond conveying assets to your heirs, as determined by the trust. Another term for this is **bare trust**. By contrast, all other trusts are **special trusts** (see below), where the trustee has active duties beyond those of a simple trust. The other meaning is in Federal income tax law, where a simple trust is one in which all net income must be distributed on an annual basis.

- ◆ **Special trust.** In the United States, a trust in which the responsibilities of the trustee extend beyond simply conveying the property to the beneficiary as determined by the trust.

- ◆ **Spendthrift trust.** A special trust in which the trustee has the authority to determine how the trust funds will be allocated to the presumably irresponsible heir.

- ◆ **Split interest trusts including GRATs, GRUTs and QPRTs.** These are trusts that provide certain income tax advantages. There are several types, including:
  - Grantor retained annuity trust (GRAT). You transfer assets to a living trust, retaining the right to a fixed annuity (payment) for a term of years, payable annually. At the end of the trust's term, the assets pass to the beneficiary. If you survive the term, the assets are excluded from your taxable estate. Alternatively, if you die during the term, the assets are included in your taxable estate.

  - Grantor retained unitrust (GRUT). Similar to a GRAT, you receive an annual payment that is determined as a percentage of the value of assets in the GRUT each year, known as a unitrust. If the assets increase in value, so do your payments.

  - Qualified personal residence trust (QPRT). A living trust that owns a personal residence for a term of years. Similar to a GRAT, you must live beyond the trust's term; otherwise the value of the personal residence is included in your taxable estate. The trust makes no payments to you during the trust's term.

  - Qualified domestic trust (QDT). The purpose is to preserve the marital deduction when the surviving spouse is not a United States citizen and the trust assets may be subject to the federal estate tax if the marital deduction is not available.

– Spousal lifetime access trust (SLAT). This is a special type of irrevocable life insurance trust (ILIT) that can permit access to life insurance cash values, while simultaneously keeping the life insurance proceeds out of your gross estate.

♦ **Standby trust, or pourover trust.** A trust that is created before death but only is provided with assets upon death, according to provisions in your will.

♦ **Unitrust.** This trust pays a variable amount each year, which is a predetermined percentage of the fair market value of the trust that year and which must be at least five percent. Contrast to an **annuity trust**, above.

♦ **Will trust or testamentary trust.** Any trust created according to instructions you have given in your will is called a testamentary trust or will trust.

## SIMON SAYS...

You should work closely with your estate planning team to determine if a trust can help you minimize tax exposure and control how your assets are distributed to your spouse, heirs, or a charitable organization.

♦

# SIMON SAYS: CHOOSE THE RIGHT TRUSTEE

◆

AS YOU PUT TOGETHER your financial legacy, you may create one or more trusts to secure and convey assets to your heirs. Chances are, the trust you create will exist long after you're gone. And while the trust's legal structure can make it impervious to change or tampering, it still needs the guiding hand of the trustee. Particularly with special trusts—those which depend upon decisions made by the trustee—the character, abilities, and attentiveness of the trustee can make big difference.

Trustees must often juggle many responsibilities. He or she may be called upon to interpret the terms of the trust, direct how the trust's assets are invested, ensure that distributions are made to your heirs, maintain financial records, and file tax returns and court reports.

The trustee is responsible for administering the trust's assets with the care and skill of a prudent person managing his or her own property. The trustee's investment choices are covered by the "prudent investor rule," which is a standard of conduct from the uniform probate code. The trustee is *not* responsible for always making profitable investments or achieving an unreasonable rate of return. If the stock market falls, so will the value of your trust.

When you create a trust, consider your trustee carefully. You may have a big pool of candidates from which to choose, because in most jurisdictions almost any competent adult can qualify to serve as a trustee. Generally, and depending on the type of trust you're establishing, your family members will be allowed to serve as trustees. Before you nominate them, check with your financial team to make sure that your friends and/or family are not disqualified from serving as trustees.

Some restrictions also apply to the naming of professional advisors, people who are not citizens of the United States, and certain institutions.

A trustee doesn't have to be a lawyer or a bank officer. You could nominate a friend, a member of your family, a corporate trustee, or a professional advisor such as an attorney or accountant.

Your chosen trustee should be not only willing, but available. A dedicated explorer who spends half the year trekking across mountain ranges may not be the best choice.

The trustee may also be a beneficiary of the trust, but you should give serious consideration to possible conflicts of interest before appointing such a trustee.

## Personal Friend

If you nominate a friend to be the trustee, his or her personal concern for and knowledge of your family can be important benefits. Your friend may be more capable than a family member of making objective decisions and resolving disputes among heirs.

One thing to consider is age. If you're eighty-five years old and your college buddy is also eighty-five, the unfortunate fact is that he or she may not live long enough to effectively oversee the trust that you create. Your trust may last for decades. If you choose a friend as trustee, you should also nominate one or more successors who can be asked to serve in case the first one cannot or does not want to serve, or passes away. If you don't name a successor trustee and one is required, the court will step in and choose one.

Another consideration is skills. If the friend lacks financial or management skills, he or she may need to hire professionals to help, which can drive up costs.

## Family Member

On a personal level, a family member may be motivated to work in the trust's best interests. He or she will already know your beneficiaries, and may not charge trustee fees. But just as with a friend who is a trustee, his or her age, financial skills, and the ability to make objective decisions are also essential.

Diplomacy is an important consideration. You want a trustee who possesses both sound judgment and good people skills, and isn't reluctant to sort out disagreements.

Before nominating any family member to be the trustee, consider very carefully the potential for conflict of interest and the exacerbation of family tensions. Trustees have the duty of undivided loyalty and the duty of no self-dealing. The duty of undivided loyalty means that regardless of the share of assets given to each of the beneficiaries, each must receive the same level of consideration and treatment. The duty of no-self dealing means that the trustee cannot take personal advantage of their situation, and when he or she is also one of the heirs, this can get sticky. Examples of self-dealing may include using trust property or connections for personal profit; selling, leasing, or borrowing trust property for the trustee's personal benefit; acting on behalf of a third party who also deals with the trust; or engaging in business that competes with the trust.

Underlying family hostility, especially involving second marriages or when one child is named a trustee for others, can linger under the surface only to erupt after your death.

# Corporate Trustee or Individual Professional Advisor

You can name an individual professional advisor, or a corporate trustee such as a bank or trust company to be your trustee. The advantages of using either a corporate trustee or professional advisor are that they can be counted on to administer the trust in an objective professional manner, and they have the knowledge and experience to do a good job. Their mission is to carry out the terms of your trust while investing the funds to maximize returns. A corporate entity, such as the trust department of your bank, also has longevity, so you do not need to worry about your beneficiaries outliving the trustee. The person who at any given time holds the position of trust officer at the bank is the person who oversees the trust.

The primary disadvantage of using a corporate trustee is the cost. Many corporate trustees and bank trust departments have minimum annual fees or fees based on a percentage of assets under management, which can eat into your legacy. Alternately, a professional advisor may charge a time-based fee to be paid by your estate.

Another potential drawback with a corporate trustee is that the trustee may not know your heirs very well. To them, the beneficiaries may be just another group of clients of the bank.

In addition, corporate trustees may have significant turnover, so as the years pass your trust may be controlled by a succession of trust administrators.

Remember that in many states you cannot name an accounting firm or a law firm as the trustee, so you would need to name an individual accountant or attorney as the trustee. Like any other individual, this person may leave the firm, requiring you to either find a new trustee or get someone else from the same firm to take over.

## A Combination

By naming co-trustees, you can give your heirs the benefits of both a personal connection and professional skills. The professional advisor or institution you designate could handle the "numbers crunching"—investments, taxes, and reporting duties. Meanwhile, your relative or friend could liaison with your heirs and respond to their individual situations. If you choose this strategy, when you set up your trust be sure to specify how the co-trustees are to resolve disputes and make decisions. Also make sure and discuss this option with the corporate trustee, because many corporate trustees do not like serving with an individual co-trustee. Either way, before naming them in your document you should interview and discuss your wishes with each of the potential trustees, and make sure they are willing to serve and that you are comfortable with them.

# Unhappy Family

Of course you want to make the right choice, and most trustees successfully serve for the trust's entire term. But on occasion beneficiaries are displeased with the trustee's performance, or there may be other issues that may call a trustee's judgement into question. To allow for this possibility, you should include a provision in your trust for removing one trustee and bringing in another. The process should be carefully structured, however, to minimize tax issues and to make sure your heirs aren't able to alter the intent of your trust. One way to do this is to require that an independent third party consent to the change of trustee.

## SIMON SAYS...

When you're setting up a trust for the benefit of your heirs, it's important to select the appropriate trustee. Consider expense, familiarity, skills, and the time frame. Work with your team, take your time, and make the best choice possible.

◆

# SIMON SAYS: CHARITABLE REMAINDER TRUSTS AND SMART TAX PLANNING

◆

PEOPLE VIEW THE IRS IN MANY WAYS, and not all of them are flattering. After all, it's the job of the IRS to take some of your money and give it to the federal government. This is an activity that does not endear the IRS to very many people other than the nation's growing army of income tax specialists.

However, the IRS has a soft spot in its heart for public charities. This is because the definition of an IRS 501(c)(3) charitable organization is that it performs a function that benefits society and that would otherwise be performed by the government. Because of this perceived redundancy, the IRS allows taxpayers to deduct from their taxable income gifts made to charitable organizations. This policy has the effect of encouraging taxpayers to make charitable donations because they get their name on the wall of the charity plus a nice tax break.

If you own a low-basis, highly appreciated asset that you would gladly sell if you could avoid paying a steep federal income tax on the proceeds (CRT), you might consider an estate planning tool known as a charitable remainder trust. This type of trust could enable you to convert an appreciated asset, such as stocks or bonds, real estate or a work of art, into an income stream for life, with a greatly reduced tax exposure.

How does it work? First, you set up your CRT. As we discussed in an earlier chapter, your trust needs a trustee to manage it. In establishing a CRT, you may name yourself as trustee, which enables you to manage the investment of the funds in the trust even though you no longer own them. You might want to review this approach with your financial advisor, as there could be reasons why this is not a good idea for your particular financial situation. By using a professional trustee such as a bank or the charity itself, you could help ensure that the arrangement complies with the complex legal rules that must be followed to retain the tax benefits.

Next, you transfer assets into the charitable remainder trust (CRT) that you have created. You may then take a charitable income tax deduction, subject to certain limitations. The trust, in turn, may sell physical assets such as fine art or real estate, and invest the proceeds into income-producing investments. Once this has been done, the CRT owns cash, stocks, bonds, and other easily liquidated funds.

As the years pass, you can get some of your money back. This is because for every year for a stated period—usually for the donor's lifetime—the trust can pay you, the donor, a certain amount of the principal and/or interest income generated by the assets of the trust. You can also name anyone else as a beneficiary—your spouse, your child, or even another charity.

At the end of the stated period, the trust is dissolved. The trust turns over the principal (also known as the "remainder" interest) to the charity named by you, the donor, in the trust agreement. The charity could be your alma mater, a museum, church, or any other qualified charitable institution.

# Tax Advantages

The tax advantages can be numerous. When the CRT sells an asset, it pays no immediate tax on the gain, so all the proceeds can be reinvested to produce income. In contrast, if you had sold the asset outright instead of giving it to the CRT, you would have paid the IRS capital gains taxes on your profit, plus any capital gains tax imposed by your state.

Suppose you own $300,000 worth of XYZ Company stock that you bought years ago for $30,000. You want to sell the low-yielding shares and invest the proceeds in US Treasury bonds. If you simply sold the stock you'd pay a 15% long-term capital gains tax, or $40,500, on the $270,000 profit. Instead, you transfer the stock into a CRT, and elect to receive $12,000 annual income for the rest of your life, at which time the principal will go to your designated charity. The trust sells the shares and buys 4% Treasuries, paying no current capital gains tax on the $300,000 gain. The yearly income stream the trust pays out to you will generally be considered distributions of ordinary income, on which you will pay tax.

Your initial $30,000 investment that you made years ago is considered your cost basis. But you do have available an income tax deduction in the year the transfer is made to the CRT. Since the stock won't pass to the charity for several years, however, the deduction will be less than the stock's current market value. The available deduction will be equal to the present value of the remainder interest given to the charity of your choice. Calculation of the deduction is based on four main factors: the fair market value of the asset, the life expectancy of the income beneficiary (the person receiving the yearly payout, which in this case is you), the discount rate, and the payout rate chosen by the income beneficiary.

How does this affect your estate taxes? Whether you choose to make a gift of an asset directly to a charity or through a CRT, the value of the asset, together with any future appreciation, will effectively be removed from your taxable estate, which can help reduce your estate tax liability at your death.

# Donating Tangible Assets: The Related Use Rule

Donating art, antiques, collectibles or other tangible personal property is subject to the related use rule, which can affect the amount of your immediate income tax charitable deduction. Donating property that you have owned for over one year usually generates a charitable deduction equal to the object's fair market value at the time of the gift, so long as the charitable institution uses the object in a manner related to its charitable purpose.

For example, donating a work of art to a museum's permanent collection would clearly meet the related use rule. But if you donate the painting to your charity of choice, which in turn sold it and used the proceeds to support other causes, this would not be a related use. If the charity does not intend to use the art work to further its charitable mission, your income tax deduction is limited to your basis (generally, what you originally paid for the object), not its current, appreciated value.

Your deduction may be similarly limited if dealing or collecting art is your business, because the artwork could be considered part of your inventory. The amount of deductions you are allowed in any one year are further limited by your adjusted gross income and the type of charitable organization to which you are contributing. Generally, gifts to public charities generate larger tax deductions than gifts to private charities.

It may be easier to meet the related use rule by giving fine art directly to a charity, instead of through a trust, thereby increasing the amount of your deduction. Using a CRT as a receptacle for a painting, for instance, will probably limit the deduction to your basis in the painting. If the CRT converts the painting into an income-producing asset, the related use test will not likely be met. Nevertheless, the CRT may still be a viable method of transferring appreciated works of art with a low cost basis from a collection in order to create a revenue flow, avoid immediate capital gains, and reduce the size of the donor's taxable estate.

## Life Insurance Policy

If you are removing significant assets from your estate, and they are not being passed to your heirs, you may want to set up a strategy to make up the difference. One way to replace assets donated to charity is by purchasing life insurance for the benefit of your heirs. The increased income resulting from the tax deduction for the donated asset together with the cash flow produced by the investment of the trust proceeds may provide enough funds to purchase the insurance policy. The policy's death benefit may be kept out of your estate, thereby reducing your estate tax bill, by holding the insurance policy in an irrevocable trust and making it the owner of the policy.

## Unitrusts and Annuity Trusts

There are two basic kinds of charitable remainder trusts. Both are irrevocable, which means they can't be cancelled once the trust document is executed.

The charitable remainder **unitrust** pays out a fixed percentage of the net fair market value of the trust assets. The unitrust pays a variable return that fluctuates with the changing value of the invested fund. For this reason, a unitrust must be revalued each year, which can drive up administrative expenses, especially with hard-to-value assets such as real estate, fine art, or closely held business interests. But under certain conditions a unitrust also permits additional contributions of property, which can increase your income. Younger investors tend to prefer a unitrust because its flexibility can help provide a hedge against inflation over the long term.

The charitable remainder **annuity trust** provides a fixed amount of income flow each year. These types of CRTs tend to be more popular with seniors who want the security of a guaranteed income in their golden years and who don't want to take the risk that a market slide could diminish their income in years to come.

The Internal Revenue Code mandates a minimum percentage value for the charity's remainder interest and limits the yearly annuity and unitrust payments from a CRT. The annual amounts received by the beneficiary are normally subject to income tax, either as ordinary income or as capital gains.

## SIMON SAYS...

When properly structured, a charitable remainder trust may effectively achieve a variety of tax and financial planning objectives that can strengthen your legacy. Ask your professional estate planning adviser about how charitable giving can be a part of your legacy.

◆

# SIMON SAYS:
# BYPASS TRUSTS

◆

L ET'S SAY YOU'RE MARRIED and, because it's possible that your spouse will outlive you, you want to provide for his or her comfort and lifestyle after you're gone. You also want to provide for your children or grandchildren after your spouse has died. The problem is that you are concerned about paying a hefty estate tax—both on your estate at your death (in trust jargon, this is the "first death"), and upon your spouse's estate upon his or her death (the "second death"). If all of the assets passed outright to the surviving spouse upon your death (the first death), they could all be subject to estate tax at the second death.

A bypass trust or credit shelter trust is an irrevocable trust used to minimize the combined estate taxes payable by spouses. By using the applicable credit amount to shelter assets at the first death, the value of the trust can escape estate taxation at the second death. The name comes from the trust assets "bypassing" the taxable estate of your surviving spouse.

One condition of a bypass trust is that the beneficiary—your surviving spouse—must have restricted rights to withdraw principal. When you create the trust, you specify how much money can be withdrawn and for what purpose.

The bypass trust usually provides that your surviving spouse will receive the income from the trust for life, with the principal then passing to the children upon the second death. During his or her lifetime, the surviving spouse usually has additional rights in the bypass trust. In addition to all the income, he or she can often have carefully limited rights over the allocation of the principal. Ordinarily, the surviving spouse cannot control the final disposition of the trust, which is dictated by the trust terms established by you.

Here's how a bypass trust works. In simple terms, upon your death, the bypass trust is funded with assets having a value equal to the maximum amount that can be transferred to a *non-spouse* (that is, the trust) without estate taxes being imposed. For tax purposes the assets placed in the bypass trust are not treated as being legally owned by the surviving spouse, and would therefore not be included in his or her estate for purposes of federal estate tax liability. Upon the surviving spouse's death, the assets are passed to the trust's beneficiaries (usually children or grandchildren) without estate tax.

Your estate can be divided to minimize tax liability. Upon your death, the instructions in your will divide your estate into two parts. One part is equal to the applicable exclusion amount sheltered from tax by the applicable credit amount, and is placed in a trust. The trust names your surviving spouse as the beneficiary, but will bypass his or her estate at death. The second part either passes outright to the surviving spouse, or is placed in a marital deduction trust for the spouse's benefit.

Not all trust income must be paid out to the surviving spouse. Instead, the trustee is given leeway to either pay out or to accumulate income, usually on the basis of the spouse's income requirements. If income is accumulated in the trust, the trust pays income tax under the special rate schedule for trusts and estates.

## Sprinkling Trust

In the sprinkling trust, the trustee is given the power to "sprinkle" income—and perhaps also principal—among several beneficiaries, such as the spouse and children. If the spouse is already in a relatively high income tax bracket, this can substantially reduce the family tax burden while still keeping all the trust income within the family unit. Sometimes it is the surviving spouse who holds the sprinkling power rather than the trustee.

Giving the trustee or surviving spouse a sprinkling power enables you to anticipate that as time goes by, certain members of your family may have more pressing financial needs than others. For example, one child may have three children, all of whom attend college, while another child may be childless.

## Other Beneficiaries

While the surviving spouse is usually the major income beneficiary of the bypass trust, this is not a requirement. If your spouse is comfortable in his or her own right, then you may want to name your children or grandchildren as beneficiaries. The same estate tax result will hold: as long as the trust does not give the beneficiary a general power of appointment over the assets of the trust, the trust will generally not be includible in the gross estate of any beneficiary who dies while the trust is in existence.

Bypass trusts should be prepared with the assistance of your lawyer or qualified estate planner, because if a bypass trust is not prepared properly the IRS will not honor it. An adverse IRS ruling can force your heirs to pay hefty estate taxes.

Tax laws can and do change. In 2010 President Obama signed the two-year Bush tax cut extension, which, among other things, included the provision that exempted estates under $10 million for couples and taxes subsequent income at 35 percent. This meant that in the new estate tax provisions, the limit on the amount that can be passed tax-free to a *non-spouse* (the trust) was increased to $5 million. In addition, the measure included the Deceased Spouse Unused Exclusion Amount (DSUEA), which directly affected how estate planners consider bypass trusts. The law allowed the executor of your estate to transfer your unused tax exemption to your surviving spouse for use in addition to your surviving spouse's estate tax exemption. It's a feature that estate planners call "portability." This made it possible for

your unused estate tax exemption to be "stacked" on top of your surviving spouse's exemption without the use of a bypass trust.

In early 2013 Congress passed changes to the tax code, and more
action was promised in the first few months of the year. The lesson is
that you need to consult with a tax specialist who is up to date on all
the changes that have happened or will happen to the federal tax code.

## SIMON SAYS...

If you want to provide for your surviving spouse and then have
your estate pass to your children, contact your lawyer or qualified
estate planner and discuss a bypass trust.

◆

# SIMON SAYS: DYNASTY TRUSTS

◆

L ET'S SAY YOU'RE THE TYPE OF PERSON who likes to consider the long term. Not just months or years long term—I mean decades and longer. When planning your legacy, you're not thinking in terms of your remaining years of life, or even the lives of your children. You're thinking about your grandchildren, great-grandchildren, and beyond.

You're either an optimist or a benevolent control freak.

The challenge to long-term planning has traditionally been this: Property rights are established under state laws, not federal law. With respect to the creation, administration, duration, and termination of trusts, property held in trust is subject to applicable state law. For most of the twentieth century, states recognized a common law called the rule against perpetuities, which limits the duration of a trust to the period of lives "in being" at the time of the trust's creation, plus twenty-one years following the last survivor's death. This means that any future interest that does not vest within this time period would be void.

The rule against perpetuities prevents a person from putting directives in his or her will that would continue to control or affect the distribution of assets long after he or she has died. This is a concept often referred to as control by the "dead hand."

For example, if at the time you create the trust, the beneficiaries include your grandchildren, the youngest of whom, Sally, is five years old. She is therefore the youngest of anyone "in being" at the time of the trust's creation. Let's say Sally lives to be eighty-five years old. The rule against perpetuities would demand that the trust be dissolved 106 years after you drafted it.

In the case of your will, the time of creation is when you die, not when you draft your will.

There has always been a "charity-to-charity" exception. For example, a conveyance "to the Museum of Art, so long as it operates as a public charity; but if it does not, then to the YMCA" would be acceptable under the rule against perpetuities because both parties are charities. Even though the interest of the YMCA might not vest for hundreds of years, the conveyance would nonetheless be held valid.

Is a lifetime plus twenty-one years not enough time for you to direct your legacy to your heirs? There is good news. Because the law can be vague and difficult to enforce, since 1995 twenty-six states have revised or repealed their laws regarding the rule against perpetuities, thus relaxing or eliminating the limitations on trust duration. Even today, state legislatures continue to revise laws concerning the rule against perpetuities and trust duration, so it's a good idea to check with your estate planner for the current laws in your state.

# What Is a Dynasty Trust?

A dynasty trust is a multi-generational trust established in a state that has revised or repealed the rule against perpetuities. When properly established and administered, a dynasty trust can conserve family wealth through successive generations by minimizing the effect of federal transfer taxes.

Like any other trust, the terms of the trust are designed to both preserve and distribute trust assets. Like a charitable remainder trust, a dynasty trust is an irrevocable trust. Neither the grantor nor any subsequent beneficiary may alter its terms. Beneficiaries are not allowed to access the trust assets, nor can they sell their beneficiary interest in the trust.

The trust defines beneficiaries by identifying existent beneficiaries (presumably family members) and specifying lineal descendants as future beneficiaries. Corporate trustees (such as a bank) are generally preferred over individuals because the corporate trustee is likely to outlive the grantor and beneficiaries. The trustee must be independent to properly execute his or her role, but can be instructed to only make discretionary distributions of income or income and principal to the beneficiaries based on a sprinkling power.

Any asset can be used to fund the trust, including life insurance. Any appreciation in the asset after its transfer to the trust will not be subject to gift or generation-skipping transfer tax (GSTT—see more below). States that allow dynasty trusts may also provide statutory protection to the trust from the grantor's creditors, and creditors of the beneficiaries.

The terms of the trust define the end point for the trust: whether the trust will end by a certain date or will be perpetual, which means the trust will last as long as the class of beneficiaries.

If you create an irrevocable trust, the assets within the trust will not be subject to the estate tax if you have not reserved any rights in or powers over the trust and its assets. Also, because the beneficiaries only have an income interest, the trust assets will not be included in any beneficiary's estate, and the trust assets avoid subsequent estate tax.

# Generation-Skipping Transfer Tax

The generation-skipping transfer tax (GSTT) imposes a tax on both outright gifts and transfers in trust to related persons more than one generation younger than the donor, such as grandchildren, or for the benefit of unrelated persons who are more than 37.5 years younger than the donor.

The law has had a convoluted history. The first version of the federal generation-skipping tax was introduced by Congress in 1976, but the approach created so many administrative problems that in 1986 Congress repealed the original version and enacted a new GSTT law. Then in 2010, like the Federal Estate Tax, the generation-skipping transfer tax was repealed. But the law that created the increases and ultimate repeal of the GSTT Exemption expired on December 31, 2010. As of this writing, on January 2, 2013, President Obama signed the American Taxpayer Relief Act (ATRA) into law, which led to the permanent extension of the laws governing estate taxes, gift taxes and generation skipping transfer taxes that were put in place by the Taxpayer Relief Act of 2010 (TRA 2010), except that the top estate tax, gift tax, and generation skipping transfer tax rate under TRA 2010 was increased to 40% from 35%. Simon Says because tax laws change, you should always get the most current information from your financial team.

## Advantages to Using a Dynasty Trust

While a key advantage to a dynasty trust is in passing significant wealth to future generations, another benefit is that a dynasty trust avoids transfer taxes. Without the impact of federal estate taxes on each generational transfer, the assets within the trust can continue to grow over the years, though it is important to remember that the trust will pay a tax on any income it generates.

Another advantage lies in the potential appreciation of assets placed within the dynasty trust over the decades. An asset is valued for transfer taxes at the time of the transfer, and as a result an asset that appreciates goes in at a lower value, and then may be allowed to grow unencumbered by further transfer tax liability. In a properly drafted trust, the amount of wealth transferred from generation to generation can be significant.

In addition, a dynasty trust is "locked in" and avoids future changes to the federal transfer tax laws. The goal is to set up a dynasty trust at a time when the federal transfer tax exemption amounts are relatively high and the GSTT rates are relatively low.

## SIMON SAYS...

If you're interested in how your legacy plays out over decades, and you want to provide for more than one future generation, learn about a dynasty trust.

◆

# SIMON SAYS:
# RESIDENCE TRUSTS

◆

W HEN PEOPLE THINK ABOUT THEIR LEGACY, and the wealth that they intend to pass on to their children and grandchildren, they often focus their attention on liquid assets—cash, securities, and the like. They may also think about treasured possessions such as jewelry, art, and furniture.

But how about the family home or condominium? Or the vacation cottage on the lake? These can often be major assets that represent a sizable chunk of a family's wealth. They deserve careful consideration and a candid conversation with your heirs.

One option is to sell the house at some time during your retirement, thereby converting its value into cash. The cash can then be placed into a trust or distributed upon your demise.

Another option is to keep the house and will it to your heirs. The goal with this choice is that you want to keep the estate tax exposure as minimal as possible. One good solution is to place the house in a residential trust.

Personal residence trusts (or PRTs) are designed to allow you to transfer your residence or second home out of your estate at a reduced gift tax value. Once the trust is funded with the house, the residence and any future appreciation of the residence is excluded from your estate.

The trust has a time limit. You place your home in the trust, but you retain the right to live in the residence for the specified period of years. At the end of that period of years, your children (or other designated beneficiaries) become the rightful owners of the residence. Thereafter, the house will no longer be a part of your taxable estate.

When placed in a trust, your residence can still have a mortgage—

you need not own it outright. To the extent the property is encumbered by a mortgage, the value of the residence transferred to the trust will be reduced for gift tax purposes.

If you are still living when your beneficiaries take possession, with their permission you could live in the house as a tenant. Or maybe it will be time to move to one of those retirement villages where everyone drives around in golf carts. The point is that once you place your house in the trust, you are no longer the owner. This is because personal residence trusts are irrevocable split interest trusts. The transfer of the residence to the trust constitutes a completed gift.

There is one caveat: if you, the grantor, die during the defined term of the residence trust, the full value of the trust property is included in your estate, as if you were the uninterrupted owner. For this reason there may be added a contingent reversionary interest during the retained term of the trust. If you die during the retained term and if there is a reversionary interest, the age of you, the grantor, now comes into the valuation of the retained interest.

Under the terms of the trust, you, the grantor, retain the right to live in the house for a number of years, rent free, after which the remainder beneficiaries of the trust (probably your children, or a nonprofit organization) become fully vested in their interest. In this way, PRTs are similar to other types of retained interest trusts with funny acronyms like GRITs, GRATs and GRUTs, which I discussed in the chapter on types of trusts and which I'll mention again in a moment.

## Retained Interest

Because the transfer of the residence to the PRT is a completed gift, for tax purposes the goal is to minimize the value of the gift. It gets more complex when you take into account something called "retained interest." Basically, retained interest means that while you relinquish ownership, you still have a legal interest in the asset. Any grantor retained interest trust (GRIT) is a trust where you, the grantor, make an irrevocable transfer of property to a trust. However, you retain some rights and/or benefits. There may be a retained interest in the form of an annuity payment (GRAT, with an "A" for annuity), annual percentage payment (GRUT, with a "U" for unitrust), or residence (QPRT, with a "Q" for qualified) for the term of the trust. When the trust expires, the remainder interest is transferred to your beneficiaries.

In the case of personal residence trusts, the trick is to arrive at a valuation of the retained interest.

The gift is valued at the fair market value of the residence, less the value of any retained interest. Therefore, if the retained interest is valued at zero, the taxable gift equals the fair market value of the residence. However, under IRS Code section 7520, if the retained interest has value, this value will be greater than zero, and the corresponding gift value is diminished.

IRS Code section 7520 values the remainder interest using measurements that include the life expectancy of you, the grantor; the term of the trust; and the 7520 rate in effect for the month of the transfer. The higher the 7520 rate and the longer the term of the trust, the lower the value of the gift.

## Qualified Personal Residence Trust (QPRT)

The regulations under IRS Code section 2702 allow for personal residence trusts and qualified personal residence trusts (QPRTs). Of the two, QPRTs are more widely used because they offer more options. Like a regular PRT, in a QPRT the grantor has a predetermined limit on the right to occupy the residence that has been placed in trust, and must forfeit ownership at the expiration of the QPRT term.

A QPRT takes advantage of certain provisions of the law to allow you to make a gift to the QPRT of your personal residence at a discounted value. This, in turn, may remove the house from your estate, reducing potential estate taxes upon your death. The discount comes into play because the trust, when it conforms to all of the requirements set forth in the regulations, is not subject to certain special valuation provisions of IRS code which limit such discounts, and the retained and remainder interests will be valued under traditional gift tax valuation rules.

For income tax purposes, a QPRT is a grantor trust. This means that during the trust term you, the grantor, can claim an income tax deduction for any real estate taxes you pay. If structured properly, the QPRT will freeze the value of the your residence at the time you create the trust and result in significant estate tax savings. When valuing the gift of a residence, the federal interest rate under IRC section 7520 is one of the main factors that influence the tax outcome. The higher the federal rate, the lower the gift value and therefore the lower the potential gift tax. On the other hand, a low federal interest rate usually results in reduced estate tax savings.

Your decision to create a QPRT requires balancing the consequences of relinquishing ownership to your beneficiaries against the potential estate tax savings, based in part on current interest rates.

## SIMON SAYS...

While personal residence trusts can seem complicated, when properly constructed by a professional they can more than pay for themselves in tax savings. Placing your first or second home in a trust for your beneficiaries is an idea worth exploring, especially if you want the residence to stay with the family for generations.

◆

# SIMON SAYS:
# THE MARITAL DEDUCTION

◆

MARRIAGE BRINGS MANY BENEFITS—family, stability, and tax considerations among them. When you are managing your assets, there's another benefit that can work in your favor at tax time: the marital deduction.

Marital deduction is a federal tax provision that allows you to give assets to your spouse with reduced or zero tax imposed upon the transfer. Spouses can transfer property between themselves without tax liability, and even some divorced couples can do it. For federal estate and gift tax purposes, there is no tax on transfers between spouses, whether during lifetime or at death.

There is no limit to the amount of the marital deduction. You can legally eliminate all estate taxes by leaving your entire estate to your surviving spouse.

It may sound like a good deal. But, as with everything in life, there is a catch, which can be expensive for your heirs.

The marital deduction only *defers* taxes. It does not *eliminate* them. Upon your spouse's death, all the assets that were transferred to your spouse will be taxed if they have remained in his or her estate. So if you hope that your children will eventually inherit these assets, they will pay the full estate tax.

## Lifetime Credit

You can work around this problem with several estate planning tools. The first is the federal lifetime credit.

It all starts with the gift tax. The IRS, knowing that people try to dodge taxes by shifting assets among friends and relatives, taxes large gifts of cash that you give directly to any individual. There is an exclusion: you are currently allowed to give any individual a total of $14,000 per year before the IRS wants you to report it. You can give your spouse, each child, your broke cousin—anyone—up to $14,000 each, every year, with no interference from the IRS.

But can you give away millions of dollars over your lifetime to hundreds of individuals? Not quite. There is an overall upper limit, called the lifetime credit.

Every person has a lifetime credit, which is also called the estate tax exemption equivalent. Generally, the federal gift and estate tax exemption equivalent amount in 2013 is $5,250,000 million. As of this writing Congress has been modifying the tax code, so every tax-payer is urged to consult his or her tax preparer or financial advisor on current tax law.

## Unified Credit

In estate planning, gift calculations can get very complicated. That's why there's the unified credit. It gets its name because the federal gift tax and estate tax have been integrated into one unified tax system.

For example, if you exceed the annual $14,000 gift tax amount in any year, you can either pay the tax on the excess or take advantage of the unified credit to avoid paying the tax. In 2012, the unified credit enables you to give away $5,250,000 during your lifetime without having to pay gift tax.

If you use the unified credit during your life, you reduce the amount available to offset the estate tax upon your death.

## Credit Shelter Trust

A common device to manage taxes and provide funds for a surviving spouse is a credit shelter trust. This trust is structured so that upon your death, the assets specified in the trust agreement are transferred to your beneficiaries named in the trust (your children). Meanwhile, your surviving spouse maintains rights to the trust assets and the income they generate during the remainder of his or her lifetime.

I discussed this concept in the chapter on bypass trusts.

With a credit shelter trust, you can set lifetime payments to your surviving spouse however you desire. Your surviving spouse can receive primarily income, supplemented by principal payments for specific purposes. Or payments can be a fixed amount or a percentage of the trust. The trustee can be given discretion to set or increase the distributions.

Payments to the remainder beneficiaries also are flexible. The trust property can be distributed to them after your surviving spouse dies, or the annual payments can continue under a formula or at the trustee's discretion.

The credit shelter trust is offset by the lifetime estate tax exemption amount. The remainder of the estate can be left to your surviving spouse under the marital deduction. This ensures that the entire estate can be used to support your spouse, the exempt amount is used, estate taxes are minimized, and the amount in the trust eventually is distributed as desired.

It is important to balance the distribution of assets. Years ago, the trust was automatically funded with assets equal to the estate tax exemption amount. With today's higher exemption amount, the trust could absorb all or most of many estates. This may result in your surviving spouse receiving few or no assets outright and having to depend on the trust for income. This may not be the wisest choice.

Let's say you're married, you have several children, and you have a $4 million estate. In your will you leave $2 million to a credit shelter trust with your spouse as the lifetime beneficiary and your children as remainder beneficiaries. Another $1 million is left outright to your spouse, and the remaining $1 million is put in a qualified terminable interest property (QTIP) trust with your spouse as beneficiary for life and the children as remainder beneficiaries. (I'll discuss QTIP trusts in another chapter.) This arrangement uses most of your current life-time exemption, leaves your spouse adequate income and access to capital, and ensures the property eventually goes where you intended.

The key to the effective transfer of wealth is to work with your estate planning professional to construct a system that provides the maximum benefits for your spouse and children, while minimizing your estate's tax exposure.

## Qualified Domestic Trust

There is an important exception to the federal gift tax marital deduction: It is only available if your receiving spouse is a citizen of the United States.

The federal estate tax marital deduction is available for bequests at death to your surviving spouse, whether or not he or she is a US citizen. However, if your surviving spouse is not a US citizen, the bequest must take the form of a specialized type of trust known as a qualified domestic trust (known as a QDT or QDOT).

The purpose of a qualified domestic trust is to preserve the marital deduction when the surviving spouse is not a United States citizen and the trust assets are likely to be subject to the federal estate tax if the marital deduction is not available.

## SIMON SAYS...

In talking to your children or your spouse about your legacy, that it's all about fairness and wise planning. Let them know there is a difference between being a beneficiary of something like a trust and actually owning it. And of course, they should work with an expert to craft their own strategies to pay only their fair share of taxes—no more and no less.

◆

# YOUR WILL

◆

# NOTES

# SIMON SAYS:
# WRITE YOUR WILL

◆

PLANNING YOUR LEGACY is a broad-based activity that touches many aspects of your life including talking with your spouse and heirs, getting professional advice, and organizing your assets. These are all ongoing processes that most people are more than willing to undertake. When doing them you're operating in the land of the living and you're involved with things that exist today.

But sooner or later—and hopefully sooner—you need to create the key document from which all else follows. It's the cornerstone of your legacy and the roadmap that will be followed not only by your heirs but by the courts.

It's your will.

Some people have no problem tackling this task; others put it off because it quite simply reminds them that their time on earth is finite. It's no fun writing, "OK folks, here's what I want to have happen to my stuff after I'm dead." It conjures up the ghastly scene from Dickens' *A Christmas Carol* when the housekeeper lugs Scrooge's bedclothes to the local peddler. No one wants that to happen.

The fact is that if Ebenezer had a proper will, the housekeeper would have had to wait for the court-approved executor to release Scrooge's estate and everything would have been nice and tidy.

Here's why you should write your will, even if your estate is modest.

If you die without a valid will, you'll become what's called intestate. That means your estate will be settled not according to your wishes, but according to the laws of your state. In most US states and other common law jurisdictions, the distribution of your assets will follow the common law of descent. Your property will go first or primarily to your spouse, and then to your children and their descendants. If there is no spouse, children, or grandchildren, the inheritance will go to your parents, then your siblings, your siblings' descendants, your grandparents, your aunts and uncles, and so on to the remote levels of kinship. If there are absolutely no heirs, your assets may be claimed by the state.

One key thing to remember is that unless you have already created trusts, if you die intestate all of your property is transferred outright to your heirs. So let's say that your estate is worth ten million dollars. Your only legal heir (not that this applies to you, but you never know) is your nephew Vinnie who lives on a houseboat with his girlfriend. Guess what? If you die without a will, it's very likely that Vinnie will be making a big deposit into his offshore account. He'll get your house, too.

Do you need an attorney to prepare your will? Not necessarily. You aren't required to hire a lawyer to prepare your will, and you can go online and find guidance. Do-it-yourself will kits are widely available online, in bookstores, and in libraries. Your state's departments of aging may also have information about free or low-cost resources for writing your will and basic estate planning.

As long as your will meets the legal requirements of your state, it's valid whether a lawyer drafted it or you wrote it yourself on a pad of paper. However, if you have a variety of assets that you want to carefully disburse, especially with one or more trusts, then you should ask an experienced advisor to provide guidance on estate-planning strategies such as living trusts. Your lawyer will know your state laws; some states, for example, have community property laws that award your surviving spouse half of your assets after you die no matter what percentage you stipulate in your will.

Should you and your spouse have a joint will or separate wills? The answer is that joint wills are not a good idea, and some states won't recognize them. In reality, you and your spouse will die at separate times and you each have personal property, so you each need your own individual will. And of course, separate wills allow for you and your spouse to address delicate issues such as ex-spouses, children from previous relationships, and property that was acquired during a previous marriage.

Here's a basic checklist to follow when you're writing your will.

◆ To be valid, your will must be written and signed while you are in sound judgment and mental capacity.

◆ The document must clearly state that it is your will.

◆ You must name an executor, who ensures your estate is distributed according to your wishes. Duties of your executor include taking inventory of property and belongings, appraising and distributing assets, paying taxes, and settling any debts. Since the role of executor can be demanding, it can be a good idea to ask the proposed executor if he or she is willing to serve.

◆ In many states it's not necessary to notarize or record your will, but doing so can safeguard against any claims that your will is invalid. You should sign your will in the presence of at least two witnesses.

◆ Social media is a part of everyday life, and you may have many online accounts. You should appoint someone you trust as an online executor. They'll take charge of closing your email accounts, social media profiles, and blogs.

Once you've completed your will, it's a good idea to periodically review it. You'll want to consider making changes if you move to a different state, the value of your assets change, you marry, divorce or remarry, the executor of your estate or one of your heirs dies, or the laws affecting your estate change.

## SIMON SAYS...

To write your will, have it reviewed by an attorney, get it notarized, and store it somewhere safe. Then sit down with your spouse or your heirs and review with them your expectations and plans for your legacy. By discussing this sensitive topic in advance, you'll be doing them and yourself a big favor.

◆

# SIMON SAYS: LIVING WILLS AND DURABLE POWER OF ATTORNEY

◆

LET'S BE HONEST: we know that we all have to die sometime. It's a plain fact of life, and if given a choice in how to go most people would want to have an active and full life, live to be a hundred, and then maybe just drop dead in a split second. One moment you're lining up the putt on the eighteenth hole, and then boom! Lights out. No pain and no unpleasant lingering.

We should all be so lucky. In reality, the human body can take time to slow down and eventually stop. During this process you may need to change your lifestyle, and you may even become incapacitated. Medical care will become an issue, and you may not be able to exercise full control over your own health care and financial decisions. Other people—your family, doctors, and lawyers—may be making some important decisions for you.

This is why you can do yourself and everyone around you a big favor and make your wishes known in advance. After all, if the time comes when your family is standing around your bedside looking at all the tubes and wires coming out of you and the doctor says, "OK, what do you folks want to do?", wouldn't it be better if they could rely upon a document that spelled out your wishes? Of course it would.

We're going to review two important documents that will allow you to state your preferences for your own medical care: the living will and the durable power of attorney. It's a good idea to prepare both. In some states, the living will and the power of attorney can be combined into a single form, which is often called an advance directive. It's simply a set of written instructions that a person creates to specify what actions should be taken for their health if they are no longer able to make decisions due to illness or incapacity.

## Living Wills

Despite the similar name, a living will bears no relation to the conventional will or living trust used to bequest assets at death. A living will is a document that describes your health care preferences in the event that you aren't able to make these decisions yourself. In a sense, it's a will that takes effect while you're still alive.

Your living will can say as much or as little as you wish about the kind of health care you hope to receive. For example, your living will could include a do not resuscitate (DNR) request. This commonly means that cardiopulmonary resuscitation (CPR) and advanced cardiac life support (ACLS) will not be performed if a valid written DNR order is present. Note, however, that your DNR request in your living will is not a legal command to health care providers. It is the physician or hospital staff member who writes a DNR "physician's order," which may be based upon the wishes previously expressed by the individual in his or her advance directive or living will, but may also be based upon the physician's judgment.

## Durable Power of Attorney for Health Care

In your living will you state your health care preferences. In this document, you appoint someone you trust to be your health care agent (can also be called a health care proxy, attorney-in-fact for health care, or surrogate) to make the necessary health care decisions for you, and to advocate for the type of care you wish to receive.

As with term "living will," the phrase "durable power of attorney" merits some explanation. Firstly, someone who is granted power of attorney need not be a lawyer. He or she can be any responsible adult. As for the word "durable," that's included for a specific reason. Under common law, an ordinary power of attorney becomes *void* if its grantor dies or becomes incapacitated because of physical injury or mental illness. In this case, you want the opposite: you want the power of attorney to become *activated* when you are incapacitated. Under a durable power of attorney, the authority of the attorney-in-fact to act and/or make decisions on your behalf continues until your death.

These two health care documents—your living will and the durable power of attorney—take effect when and if your doctor determines that you lack the capacity to make your own health care decisions. If there is some question about your ability to communicate clearly and understand your treatment choices, your doctor (in consultation with your health care agent and/or close relatives) will decide whether it's time for your health care documents to become effective.

These documents will not give your agent the authority to override your medical care choices if you have the ability to do so. You can change or revoke a health care document at any time. If someone questions the validity of your health care directives and your health care becomes the subject of a dispute, a court may decide who prevails.

Getting a divorce does not affect your written directions for health care. But if you named your spouse as your health care agent, in a number of states his or her authority is automatically revoked and you need to name someone else as your agent.

After your death, in some states, your health care directives remain effective for limited purposes including the disposition of your body and organ donation.

## SIMON SAYS...

You should consider every end-of-life possibility, and think about how you would want to be cared for in the event of an incapacitating illness. Once you're sick it may be too late to make your wishes known, so contact your estate planning advisor or attorney and create your living will and a durable power of attorney.

◆

# SIMON SAYS:
# FINANCIAL POWER
# OF ATTORNEY

◆

W E'VE DISCUSSED YOUR LIVING WILL and the durable power of attorney for health care. These documents have carefully defined limits, and they generally do not address financial issues. In most states, to ask someone to take over your personal finances or some portion of them requires a separate document.

A financial power of attorney (FPOA) is a written document through which you (the principal) appoint and authorize another competent adult (the attorney-in-fact, or AIF), to act on your behalf in financial, business, personal, and real estate matters. The agent must act at all times in your best interests, and must act loyally, avoid conflicts of interest, cooperate with your health care providers, and keep accurate records of acts performed under the power of attorney. You can amend or revoke the FPOA at any time.

You can draft your power of attorney to give your agent any or all of these powers:

◆ Conduct your financial affairs.

◆ Manage your investments.

◆ Exercise your legal rights and conduct lawsuits.

◆ Pay your bills, such as the rent or mortgage.

◆ Apply for public benefits on your behalf.

◆ Hire caregivers for you.

◆ Make residence decisions for you.

In most jurisdictions, powers of attorney are limited by law. Most people intend for a FPOA agent to handle their day-to-day affairs, but not to make changes to their estate plan or legacy. Consequently, there are certain things your agent cannot do unless you specifically give instructions that they can do them. These specific powers include:

♦ Appointing another person as an alternate or successor agent.

♦ Paying the agent out of your funds, or making gifts or loans with your money to the agent.

♦ Creating or changing rights of survivorship.

♦ Creating or changing a beneficiary designation.

♦ Creating, amending, revoking, or terminating a trust.

♦ Delegating authority granted under a power of attorney.

♦ Buying or selling your real estate.

♦ Making gifts or loans of your money to a third party.

♦ Exercise powers, rights, or authority as a partner, member, or manager of a partnership.

♦ There are certain things that your agent or AIF can never do, even with your consent. They include:

♦ Execute, revoke, or modify a will or living will for you.

♦ Act against your instructions.

♦ Make health care decisions as part of a financial power of attorney document. This can only be done with an advance directive or durable power of attorney for health care. Your health care agent can be the same person as your financial agent; you just need two documents to do that.

A limited power of attorney, also known as a special power of attorney, is used when you want to grant to the agent only certain precisely defined powers. For example, if you're entering public office you may want to give a limited power of attorney to an advisor who will manage your investments, but not have any authority over your day-to-day finances.

## Conservators and Guardians

It's worthwhile to take a moment to clarify two other terms that you may have heard. A conservator is someone appointed by the court to make financial decisions for a protected or incapacitated person. The conservator has broad powers that may include making investments, paying bills, and performing other financial functions, as well as engaging in estate planning, and even amending or revoking the protected person's will. With the court's permission the conservator may purchase or sell real property or otherwise dispose of assets.

A guardian is appointed by the court to perform duties related to personal care, custody, and control. The court-appointed guardian can decide where the ward will live and what medical treatment he or she will receive.

## Creating a Power of Attorney

Any competent adult can create a power of attorney by writing down the name of the person he or she wishes to designate as an agent, and including exactly what he or she wants the agent to do. It should be written by an attorney to assure that your intentions are clearly expressed. Once the document has been prepared, it should then be notarized.

If you choose not to have an attorney assist you, you will find power of attorney forms available at local office supplies stores and online.

# Springing Power and Standing Power

The terms of a power of attorney will determine when it takes effect. In general, a power of attorney may take effect in two different ways.

1.  Springing power. This means that the power of attorney will take effect only when an event described in the instrument takes place. For a politician, a financial power of attorney could become active when the politician takes office. For a durable power of attorney for heath care, the event would be when your physician determines that you are incapacitated.

2.  Standing power. The power of attorney takes effect as soon as you sign it.

Remember, granting or assigning a power of attorney does not take away your rights to make decisions. An agent simply has the power to act along with you in accordance with the authorization set forth in the document. Only a court, through a guardianship and/or conservatorship proceeding, can take away your rights.

## SIMON SAYS...

The better informed you are, the better choices you will make for yourself, your family, and your legacy. You may never need to ask someone to assume financial power of attorney, but it's good to know that you have the option to step away and take a break from managing your financial affairs.

◆

# SIMON SAYS: PRESERVE FAMILY HARMONY

◆

REMEMBER WHEN YOU WERE A LITTLE KID and you went to a friend's birthday party, and maybe your friend got the cool new toy that you couldn't get? Or if your brother or sister got some special gift that you didn't receive? You probably stewed about the injustice for a while and then forgot about it. Or maybe you filed it away in the bottom of your heart and vowed never to be shortchanged again.

Now fast forward to the present. You're grown now, and you're thinking about your heirs. They could include your spouse, your children or grandchildren, favorite charities, and even your beloved pet. Sure, everyone gets along, but you remember how easily feelings can be aroused. When magnified in an adult, the sense of hurt felt by a little kid who feels left out can become bitter and lead to serious family conflict. We've all heard stories about vicious family infighting—lawsuits and recrimination—that can erupt over the division of an estate. Hearing such stories might even tempt you to leave all your assets to a shelter for stray dogs. But then again, you know that if you did that your angry heirs would sue your estate.

You don't want that—you want everyone to be happy! So how do you leave your legacy and at the same time preserve family harmony? Simon Says to follow these simple guidelines, and you'll be much more likely to pass your legacy to your loved ones in a way that keeps the peace and fosters a sense of appreciation.

1. **Avoid surprises**. Communicate to your heirs your overall intentions. If everyone in the family knows the broad outlines of your

bequests, they'll have a better understanding of your choices. Even if they don't agree or if they have concerns, they'll have had time to get used to the idea and ask questions. They're more likely to respect your choices and not try to dispute them or seek a solution through a lawsuit.

If you keep your plans under wraps, there could be arguments, confusion, and possibly court fights. If, for example, you have a special charity to which you are giving a big chunk of your estate, you need to make this clear well in advance, and it would be a good idea to make the effort to show your heirs why this charity is important to you. Or if you have a valuable work of art that obviously cannot be divided and must go to one person or to a museum, then try to explain—in your will at the very least, and in advance if possible—why a particular individual or institution should get this work of art.

2. **Plan your legacy carefully**. If you don't have a will, chaos can result, and the court will have to step in. Estate planning is critical because it's the chance for you to ensure that your possessions pass into the hands of your loved ones with the least possible administration and tax costs. Experts estimate that up to seventy percent of the population haven't created a will. Many people procrastinate, and those who have wills either haven't updated them in years or, worse, have tried to do it themselves. Do-it-yourself will kits can be risky. People don't always know the right questions to ask or the right information to include. An attorney is going to look at the totality of your estate and determine if there are missing areas that need to be addressed.

3. **Be mindful of simmering feuds**. You may love your kids equally, but unfortunately some adult children don't trust their brothers or sisters. Those suspicions can be magnified when the

child who has been acting as your caregiver has had access to your checking account. After your death, another child, who perhaps lives out of town or was not involved in your daily care, might believe that you've been raiding the piggybank.

Sometimes your kids may think it's unfair that you leave each one an equal cash gift. One of the children may have already received money for a down payment on a house or college tuition that hasn't been paid back. Now that child gets that money plus his or her portion of your estate, and the other kids may be upset. These are issues that you should probe for while you're still in charge, and you can be alerted to potential problems.

4. **Be very specific in your will**. Family heirlooms or items that have special significance, such family photos or jewelry, can cause big problems. Don't just say, "I leave my personal possessions to Jimmy." Does the phrase include your mother's ten-thousand-dollar diamond engagement ring? It will take a battery of lawyers to figure out what "my personal possessions" means. If the sentimental or valuable item isn't specifically mentioned in your will as to who gets it, don't assume that your children will be able to work it out. You can inadvertently create animosity that builds in the family and never gets relieved.

Here's one solution: distribute items and heirlooms before you die. If you don't actually deliver the item, make sure your heirs know who gets what. You can even ask for their opinions. If you have a singular artifact, such as a work of art, you can say to your heirs, "We've got this one very valuable Picasso etching. Who wants it—and why? Or should I give it to the museum?" Have an open discussion and encourage your heirs to be honest.

## SIMON SAYS...

The key is to be proactive. Take action now. Don't put it off.

Most people wait until it's too late to make their will. Find someone you can trust who will guide you through the process. Most attorneys can draft wills, but you're better off selecting an attorney who specializes in estate planning and has had experience doing it.

Consider making gifts to your heirs during your lifetime. It's more difficult to challenge your gifts while you're still alive, and there will be less to squabble over when the family gathers in the lawyer's office for the reading of your will. You may want to schedule a family meeting with your attorney and other trusted advisors to explain to your children that you have completed an estate plan because you care about them.

Sometimes there's just no easy answer and you have to say, "This is what I want to do." But if you say it before you die, you may save your estate from some big headaches and help preserve family harmony.

◆

# SIMON SAYS:
# PREPARE FOR
# UNHAPPY HEIRS

◆

WE LIKE TO THINK THE BEST OF PEOPLE. We especially like to think the best of our own family. We hope that when we pass on—as we know we must—our spouse, children, grandchildren, and other family members will have positive memories of us and will feel gratitude for our bequests to them, whether they are modest or extravagant.

You're not going to be around when your will is read, or as your investments create income in the trusts you have created. You're not going to know for sure how everyone will respond to your last wishes. Will people be unhappy? Will there be squabbling? Will an heir or heirs sue the estate or the trustee?

It's happened before and it'll happen again. Here are some of the problems faced by trustees.

An heir who is on shaky financial ground and either desperate about the need to draw on a trust or worried that its investments are dwindling may pressure the trustee. They may demand a change in investment strategies or even sue for a dissolution of the trust and a quick payout of the principle—although success with the latter idea is rare. In either case, it's a headache for the trustee.

An unhappy heir may call a series of meetings with other family members and trustees, and ratchet up the tension. In many cases, the most unreasonable heirs are the ones who are distantly related to the deceased. The more remote they are, the more likely it is that they have been "out of the loop" and have an unrealistic idea of the value of your estate.

Some heirs have a very simplistic view of trusts. They don't fully understand the temporal element of a trust, or the fact that the trust may have conditions. If you set up an educational trust to pay the college tuition of future generations, a childless heir may resent what he or she perceives to be a personal slight.

# What Can Happen?

Here's an example of a well known case involving a challenge to trustees.

Three heirs to the fortune of William Randolph Hearst claimed that the Hearst Family Trust treated them unfairly. In Hearst v. Ganzi, the plaintiffs wanted the judge in Los Angeles Superior Court to declare that they could maintain an action for breach of fiduciary duties against the trustees without violating the no-contest clause in their grandfather's will.

Here's why they wanted to sue. Sometime around the year 2040, after the death of the last of the many heirs who were alive at the time of the media magnate's death in 1951, the trust will terminate and the assets will be distributed among the remaining beneficiaries. This means that there are present income beneficiaries—including the three plaintiffs—as well as numerous future remainder beneficiaries.

In their action, the three plaintiffs contended that the trustees had breached their fiduciary duties by distributing less than 1.3 percent of the value of the common stock to the present income beneficiaries annually between 2000 and 2002. Because those distributions represented significantly less than the income normally earned on trust investments, the plaintiffs asserted, the trustees were favoring the future remainder beneficiaries over the current income beneficiaries.

Unfortunately for the plaintiffs, Hearst's will provides that, among other things:

"If any person who is or would be a ... beneficiary of a trust created herein or hereunder ... directly or indirectly shall institute or participate or cooperate in the institution or filing or prosecution of any proceeding or proceedings of [any] kind or character whatsoever tending in any manner or to any extent to change, annul, revoke, set aside or invalidate this my Will or any of its provisions, including but not limited to any trust created herein or hereunder or any of the provisions of any such trust . . . , then and in any such event I hereby revoke and annul all bequests, devises and provisions made or interest created in or under this my Will for any such person."

The three heirs lost their case. The Court of Appeal agreed with the trial judge that their action, if carried forward, would violate the no-contest clause. The judge noted that the trustees were not being accused of fraud or gross neglect, or of discriminating against the income beneficiaries based on personal animus or some other consideration. Under that circumstance, the presiding justice said, the court must defer to the intent of the testator.

## Take Steps to Keep the Peace

Here's what you can do to help ensure that your wishes are carried out, family harmony is preserved, and your faithful executor or trustee doesn't get harassed or sued by an unhappy heir.

◆ Diminish any sense of entitlement. The term "trust fund baby" may be a cliché, but some heirs believe they are owed something. You can get a feeling for this sentiment by communicating the gist of your bequests while you're still able to act as the family referee. Let your heirs know what they can expect (or not expect) in general terms. It's better, of course, to downplay expectations. Tell your family not to expect life-changing deposits into their bank accounts. With the possible exception of your spouse if he or she were not the primary breadwinner, your heirs need to know that they are responsible for their own lives and that it's not a good idea to expect a windfall. You may also make it clear, for example, that you're setting up a family trust whose income will be used strictly for paying college tuition. Get people used to the idea before it becomes a reality.

◆ Choose your trustee wisely. Professional trustees have experience in dealing with the demands of heirs, and are more likely to keep a cool head. They know that providing a rational explanation of why something can't happen often makes the agitated person calm down and eventually fade away.

They know that openly fighting with a client can escalate tensions. In the vast majority of cases everyone must follow the dictates of your will and the trusts you create, and that an angry heir may simply not have the legal leverage to get what he or she wants.

Trust officers at a financial institution are trained to listen, collect information, and proceed judiciously. They may take the heir's request—for example, to make an unscheduled withdrawal of cash—to a committee, which is charged with reviewing the request and deciding whether it's consistent with rules of the trust.

◆ Use "in terrorem." No, it's not a Stephen King novel. "In terrorem" (also known as a forfeiture clause) is Latin for a legal command that you can write into your will. It says that anyone who contests your will is required to forfeit whatever bequest has been granted to him or her. Hence the terror of trying to get more, only to end up with nothing.

But an in terrorem clause is not absolute and does not eliminate all chances of a challenge. In most states a legal attack on a will is allowed to proceed if the challenge is deemed by the court to be in good faith and there is probable cause. On the other hand, an in terrorem clause may prevail if the challenge is deemed to be a frivolous or nuisance suit designed to extort more money from the rightful beneficiaries.

Why are wills challenged? Unhappy or potential heirs may believe that you, the testator, were unduly influenced by a beneficiary (usually a new spouse or doting caregiver) or that you were suffering from diminished capacity at the time the will was written and you didn't really know what you were doing.

An effective way to deflect a challenge is to do what tort lawyers do every day: essentially buy off a disgruntled heir by leaving him or her something of value so that he or she will take what is on the table rather than file a lawsuit and risk the uncertain outcome of litigation.

This can be used in combination with proactive communication. Be entirely frank with your heirs and let them know what to expect, so there will be no unpleasant surprises or disappointment when your will is read.

## SIMON SAYS...

If a potential heir is to be left little or nothing, you should state that fact clearly in your will, and you might even include a statement explaining that you have adequately provided for the heir during his or her lifetime, or that you are leaving the heir some small amount, or even that the heir is to receive nothing for a very good reason that you can either imply or state outright.

## SIMON SAYS...

The key is to inoculate your will against charges that when you wrote your will you were incapacitated or under the influence of another beneficiary.

◆

# SIMON SAYS:
# CHOOSE YOUR EXECUTOR

◆

ONE OF THE THINGS that may make you put off or delay writing your will is the knowledge that after you die, your property will be in the hands of other people. These folks will be your heirs as well as other people who may come out of the woodwork to claim part of your estate. The courts may be involved, and lawyers too. Throughout the process you're not going to be there to defend or explain yourself. It will be out of your hands.

The best way to see that your wishes are carried out, of course, is with a detailed and properly witnessed will. The other key element is the person or people whom you have entrusted to oversee the disposition of your estate—your executor.

Choosing an appropriate executor is important. To make the best choice, we need to start with the basics, and learn about the functions of your executor and what you can expect from him or her.

In the simplest sense, your executor is charged with protecting your property until all debts and taxes have been paid, and then seeing that the remainder is transferred to the people who are entitled to it.

The law does not require your executor to be a lawyer or financial expert, but it does require "fiduciary duty," which is honesty, impartiality, and diligence. The executor must act with scrupulous good faith on your behalf.

Your executor has a number of duties, which include:

◆ Identify and secure your assets, and manage them until they are distributed to your heirs. This may include deciding whether to sell securities or real estate.

◆ Determine who inherits your property. The executor will read your will to determine asset distribution. (And of course, having read this book, you will have created a valid will.)

◆ File your will in the local probate court. Generally, this step is required by law, because the function of the probate court is to affirm that your will is a legitimate document.

◆ Manage the details. This may include terminating credit cards and leases, closing bank accounts, and notifying government agencies such as Medicare, the Social Security Administration, and the Post Office of your passing.

◆ Open a bank account to receive funds that may be owed to your estate, such as paychecks, insurance payments, or dividend payments.

◆ Pay debts and taxes. Your estate may need to file a final income tax return, covering the period from the beginning of the tax year to the date of your death. State and federal estate tax returns may be required for large estates.

◆ Pay expenses such as mortgage, utility bills, and homeowner's insurance premiums.

◆ Oversee the distribution of your property as stipulated in your will or as required under state law.

◆ Comply with all current state and federal tax law. It may be that your surviving spouse can carry over any part of the federal estate tax exclusion not used by you before you died. To take advantage of "portability," as it is called, your executor needs to transfer the unused exclusion to your surviving spouse, who can then use it to make lifetime gifts or pass assets through his or her estate. The prerequisite is filing an estate tax return within nine months after your death (a six-month extension may be allowed). If the executor does not file the return or misses the deadline, your surviving spouse may lose the right to portability.

# Whom Should You Choose?

Your choice of executor can mean the difference between your estate either being settled smoothly and efficiently or getting tangled up in legal and financial knots. Your executor should not only be honest and diplomatic, but also good with paperwork, well organized, and scrupulous about meeting deadlines.

You may instinctively think of naming a family member, especially your spouse or a child. The assumption is that your close relative understands your intentions, knows your house and your assets, and can find the property that needs to be inventoried.

One basic consideration is the executor's location. Duties of the executor, including court appearances, property maintenance, and checking the mail, can be very difficult if the executor doesn't live in your home city. Ideally you'll want someone who is able to "make the rounds" on a regular basis. In addition, some states have regulations restricting out-of-state executors, so if you're considering someone who lives across the state line—even five miles away—check your state laws.

In the absence of a family member, then you'll have to go with a trusted friend or colleague. And of course your executor, whether family member or friend, can always call an expert when their own knowledge isn't sufficient. This is why you might want to consider a professional individual such as a lawyer or accountant, or a corporate fiduciary like a bank or trust company. But given the rapid changes in the financial marketplace, you may choose not to name a specific bank or trust company in your will, but rather appoint someone you trust to interview trust companies and then select one that's a good fit.

Don't name all of your children as co-executors. Either they're going to squabble or one child will end up doing all the work anyway. Plus if you name, for example, four people as co-executors, then every document will need all four signatures. This is a burden on them and a recipe for disaster. It's better to name just one child, and to make the others alternates.

Costs can vary. When family members serve as executors, they often forgo the fees even though they can still be reimbursed for travel and other expenses directly related to their duties. Many states set limits on the fees that executors may charge. Some caps are formulated in terms of what's reasonable, while others are based on a percentage of the value of the property that goes through probate.

## SIMON SAYS...

One key thing to remember is that before you name someone as executor, talk to them! Make sure that person is willing to serve. Some people are simply unwilling to take on the responsibility, or may have family or business demands that would make it difficult. And once your decision is made, communicate this to the other family members you did not choose, lest they feel overlooked. The more thoroughly you do the advance work, the more smoothly the process will unfold.

◆

# SIMON SAYS: PROVIDE THE INFORMATION NEEDED BY YOUR HEIRS AND EXECUTOR

◆

IT MAY BE TEMPTING TO THINK that writing your will and making generous arrangements for your heirs, either through bequests or trusts, is all you have to do to pass on your asset legacy. That may have been true in a simpler time a century ago, but nowadays even people of modest means have lives that are increasingly complex. We are likely to own a variety of assets that need documentation, such as houses, cars, and securities. We are likely to have one or more bank accounts, utility accounts, cell phones, insurance policies, credit cards, loans, medical accounts, and more. Most of these are private and may be protected by passwords. Their very existence may not be known to anyone but you.

Of course, after you're gone, sorting out all of these assets and accounts isn't your concern. That's why it may be tempting to brush it off and assume that your executor, the courts, and your heirs will get everything figured out. But there are two big problems with this approach.

The first problem is that it simply isn't fair. While you may be making generous gifts as a part of your legacy, asking your executor and your heirs to play detective and untangle your personal property can be time consuming and costly. They're probably going to be grief-stricken and worried more about arranging your funeral than finding the old deed to the lakefront cottage.

The second problem is that if the court has to step in and make determinations, your wishes may not be followed as explicitly as you had hoped. The more ambiguity and incompleteness there is in your legacy package, the greater chance exists that something will be overlooked or misappropriated.

In order to facilitate as smooth a transition as possible, you owe it to yourself and your heirs to get organized and make sure that your entire tangible legacy is accessible and easy to identify. Here are some key documents that you'll need to create or have as part of a legacy package.

1. **Keep your will up to date.** Did you write and sign your will ten years ago? It probably needs to be updated. An old will that does not reflect your current situation slows down the process and adds to the confusion. Once you've updated your will, don't store the original copy in your safe deposit box. Unless you've make the safe deposit box information and key readily available, your heirs may not know where it is or be able to gain access to it immediately after your death.

2. **Include an ethical will.** Once you've described how you want your tangible assets to be distributed, you may also want to create an ethical will. These can take many forms—you can express your feelings towards close family members, share your values and tell your personal or family history, or explain your estate planning decisions. It's a very useful tool, and the format doesn't matter— you can make a video, write it in your own hand, or type it on the computer. It's all about adding clarity and a personal touch to your legal will. And, just like your legal will, make sure it's easily accessible.

3. **Keep your beneficiaries updated.** You probably chose your beneficiaries when you first wrote your will, opened an investment account, bought insurance, or started a new job. Many assets such

as retirement plans, insurance policies, and individual retirement accounts require that a beneficiary be designated. You may have done this many years ago, and since that time life may have changed. You need to make sure that none of your beneficiaries have passed away or are otherwise out of the picture; and on the other side of the coin, the grandchild who was a minor ten years ago may now be an independent adult. Keep a dated record of your beneficiary designations so that your beneficiaries are aware of your intent and you know exactly where your assets will be going.

4. **Create one authoritative resource.** Putting your personal information in one place helps your executor and your heirs make important decisions quickly and efficiently. Keep this list or package in an obvious and easy-to-find place, like the top drawer of your desk.

   Here are the key items you should include.

   ◆ **Contact list.** You probably have an address book or computer file with the names and addresses of relatives, friends, and business associates. Make sure it is easily accessible and not password protected. If it's a computer file, print out a hard copy along with the file address.

   ◆ **Key documents list.** Make an inventory of all the original documents and files your heirs will need to locate. Include your birth certificate, marriage certificates and/or prenuptial and divorce agreements, updated will, durable powers of attorney, insurance policies, trust documents, real estate deeds, mortgages, auto titles, passport, health care proxies, and military discharge form. The actual documents may be kept in a safe deposit box or your attorney's office, but make sure that they'll be accessible.

◆ **Valuables list.** These are the tangible assets that you own including jewelry, fine art, furniture, cars, heirlooms, and any other personal property that's part of your estate. From a monetary perspective these items may not necessarily be valuable. But for all financially valuable assets, it's a good idea to provide an exact written description, a photograph, or a recent appraisal for insurance purposes. The goal is to avoid ambiguity. Be as clear as you can.

◆ **Net worth statement.** Every financial asset that you either own or owe should be listed. Provide a detailed description that identifies the financial institution and the account numbers. Credit cards, loans, mortgages, trusts, and checking and savings accounts should all be included. If you use online banking or bill paying, list the websites and passwords. If you're the head of a functioning household, you'll also want to provide a list of utility companies and how you pay the bills—online or by mail. Provide a clear description of where your tax records, investment statements, and other primary data files are located.

◆ **Last wishes.** You have every right to express what you want for your final arrangements. If you're highly organized you may have already made arrangements with a funeral home and a cemetery. Whether or not you've been that proactive, discuss what type of funeral you would like and any special requests. Indicate if you want your body to be available for organ donations or medical research. Let your heirs know if, for example, you want to be cremated and your ashes scattered in a special place. This is a discussion that you hopefully will have in person—but also put it in writing.

5. **Divest before you die.** The more stuff you get rid of while you're alive, the less stuff there will be for your heirs to worry about. If

you have grown children, ask them to remove their childhood possessions from the house. Being mindful of gift tax limitations, give away heirlooms and jewelry so that you can personally ensure that your chosen heirs receive the assets that you intend for them.

6. **Have cash on hand**. Ensure that sufficient liquid assets are available while your estate is being settled. Even after your death, those regular monthly bills will still need to be paid.

## SIMON SAYS...

If you sincerely want to both benefit your heirs and ensure that your wishes are followed, be proactive. Get organized. Pretend that you're a family member or executor who needs to manage your estate after you're gone. Is there clarity? Are your assets accessible? Can your wishes be challenged? Will your heirs be socked with a big tax bill because you did not use appropriate divestiture strategies? Protect your legacy by creating a strong and transparent plan for your heirs to follow.

◆

# SIMON SAYS: MANAGE YOUR DIGITAL LEGACY

◆

IN 1980, THIS CHAPTER could not have been written. The idea of digital property did not exist.

But now we're in the digital world, and even the most traditional of folks have an online presence including social media sites, bank accounts, retail accounts, and email accounts.

And, back in 1980, all of your important documents were on paper. You kept them in a safe deposit box, along with your jewels and savings bonds. Today, much of that information is online and guarded by lots of passwords. Think of the trouble *you* have remembering all those passwords. After you die, just imagine what your heirs will face if you don't make the information readily available.

What sorts of digital accounts are you likely to have? Your list may include:

◆ Social media sites.

◆ Utilities including phone, electric, or gas.

◆ Credit cards.

◆ Bank accounts including savings and checking.

◆ Brokerage and securities trading accounts.

◆ Government accounts including tax, healthcare, Medicare.

◆ Financial accounts including car and home insurance.

◆ Loan payment accounts including car and mortgage.

◆ Retail store accounts.

◆ Your own website or blog.

◆ Websites for hobbies, special interests, social clubs, and subscriptions.

◆ If you haven't yet retired, your employer probably has a password-protected intranet.

◆ The Internet has made more choices available for finance and estate planning, and attorneys often store wills and trusts online.

What should you do? List everything you have online including bank accounts, tax returns, trust documents, life insurance, wills, real estate deeds, and investment and retirement documents. You may have more online accounts than you imagine—many people including senior citizens now conduct banking and investment transactions, file tax returns, and pay bills online.

You can save your relatives, heirs and executor considerable time and effort if you follow these steps to organize your online accounts.

1. Name your durable power of attorney. In case you become incapacitated, this person will need your account information and passwords so that he or she can go online to pay bills, maintain your email box, and monitor your accounts.

2. Create an inventory. In the chapter on making information available to your durable power of attorney, heirs and executor, we cover this in detail. Provide a list of your online accounts and their passwords. Don't forget to identify your digital assets that live on your personal devices. Create a complete list of all the computers, external drives and other hardware devices that may contain materials your heirs or executor will need. Describing the location of your digital assets will enable your heirs to manage the full range of your digital estate.

3. Keep a record of monthly bills that you pay manually as well as those that are automatically deducted from your accounts. Don't

forget to list automatic bill pay for services and products such as subscriptions or online clubs.

After your death, financial institutions will not allow access to your accounts until a death certificate is presented and the executor is named. When this happens the accounts are transferred to the executor or a new account is created in the name of the estate. In this case the executor has less need for your passwords, but he or she must have a list of your accounts so the institutions can be notified and the probate process simplified.

## Online Safety Deposit Boxes

As if there weren't enough online options, an alternative to the physical list or inventory is an online safety deposit box that stores information and passwords about your online accounts or assets, with instructions detailing who should be notified in the event of your incapacitation or death.

These services let you create an account, enter all your online assets, and name a beneficiary for each asset. It can help you to store and organize important documents, such as your will and tax returns. When the service verifies proof of your death, it sends an email to the listed beneficiaries and allows them to have access.

It's confidential. The idea is similar to a Swiss bank account— once you open your account, it's private. No one but you knows what you put in there.

Likewise, digital estate planning focuses on identifying all of your online accounts, tools, and services that are part of your digital legacy. Bookmark sites that should be included in your planning. They include obvious entities such as online businesses, financial and merchant accounts, social media, email, blogs, and also online storage accounts, web hosting information, domain names you may own, online gaming sites you patronize, and any other online activity or service that should be included in your digital estate.

Having a secure, accessible and designated place for any asset or document that can be represented in digital form is a good idea. I invite you to visit www.saulsimon.com for information about setting up a cloud-based lockbox for all of your assets and legal documents.

## Memorial Websites

Here's another idea you may want to discuss with your heirs: in the past several years there's been a significant growth in memorial websites. Offered by various online services, the basic page is often free, while upgrades come at a fee. Your heirs can assemble photos, videos, your life story, and anything else that's uploadable, and in a few minutes create a lasting Internet memorial to you, with its very own URL. It's an interesting idea, but for it to work your heirs will need access to photos and other documents that may come from your estate.

## Bequeath or Delete?

Documenting your digital estate includes providing instructions for how you want your digital estate to be managed. You'll want to differentiate between online accounts that are simply bill-paying tools and those that have some intrinsic value. The former can be deleted as part of the estate settlement process; the latter may be included in your estate.

You may wish to specify which items or accounts be preserved, deleted, bequeathed, or donated; and which items should be delivered to which trustee, friend or loved one. Perhaps, if it is substantial, you may wish to consider donation of your digital legacy to a local archive or historical society.

Don't forget to authorize your digital executor in your legal will. It can be the same person as your primary executor, or you can identify a separate digital executor to handle your digital affairs.

## SIMON SAYS...

Digital estate planning should be an essential part of your legacy. Because of the ephemeral nature of our digital property—they're just electrons, aren't they?—it's easy to overlook how we have grown to depend upon the Internet to manage our assets, and the fact that in those uncounted billions of electrons there may be significant value that we can, and should, pass on to our heirs.

◆

# Thank You

◆

I HOPE THAT THIS BOOK HAS BEEN HELPFUL to you. At Simon Financial Group, our goal is to provide you with an objective fee-based financial plan designed for the unique needs of you and your heirs. The process begins with your personal financial planner collecting all of the necessary data about you and your objectives. We then take that data, analyze it, and produce a plan that has specific findings and recommendations regarding your current situation and what needs to be done to help you achieve your goals. We'll review with you the solutions that can be used to implement your plan and help you every step of the way towards a bright future for you and your heirs.

For more information about how we can assist you, I invite you to contact me today. I look forward to hearing from you.

**Saul M. Simon**, CFP®, CFS, RFC
Simon Financial Group
333 Thornall Street Suite 9B
Edison, NJ 08837
Toll Free: 888.SIMON.SAYS / 888.746.6672
Phone: 732.623.2070
Fax: 732.623.2088
Web: www.SaulSimon.com
Email: Simonsays@LFG.com
Twitter: @888Simonsays

Made in the USA
Charleston, SC
13 November 2013